Brand Protection & Leveraging Strategies for Creatives, Techies & Entrepreneurs

Christine C. Washington, Esq. LL.M. IP

www.MarksForMusicMoviesAndMore.com

ISBN: 978-0-692-91583-7

LCCN: 2017910595

10 9 8 7 6 5 4 3 2 1

DISCLAIMER:

THE INSIGHT AND OPINIONS THAT FOLLOW ARE NOT A SUBSTITUTE FOR OBTAINING PERSONAL AND SPECIFIC LEGAL ADVICE REGARDING YOUR PARTICULAR MATTER. (THIS BOOK IS NOT A DO-IT-YOURSELF MANUAL.)

THERE'S A LAWYER FOR EVERY BUDGET; PLEASE DEVELOP AN ONGOING RELATIONSHIP WITH ONE WHO IS KNOWLEDGEABLE ABOUT THE SUBJECT MATTER AND USE THE WORDS THAT FOLLOW AS A GUIDE AND REFERENCE TOOL – A "HOMEWORK" ASSIGNMENT PRIOR TO MEETINGS AND CALLS.

"THE 'OXFORD COMMA' IS AN <u>OPTIONAL</u> COMMA

"

. . .

~ THE OXFORD DICTIONARY

DEDICATION

To creators and inventors the world over: you really are the only reason that we're still evolving, intellectually, as a species. (Don't let anyone smother your passion or shade your vision.)

Mom - for sharing your love of the written word and Dad - for *insisting* on that 11th grade typing/word processing class, I dedicate my first book to the two of you.

"GOOD **NAME** IN MAN AND WOMAN ...
IS THE IMMEDIATE JEWEL OF THEIR SOULS ..."

~ William Shakespeare
Othello, Act III, Scene 3

CONTENTS

ACKNOWLEDGMENTS

Thank you to everyone who has ever sought and accepted my advice and entrusted me with the care of their most precious (inanimate) assets: their names, ideas and dreams. You continue to inspire me.

Twenty years of heartfelt thanks is also owed to legal colleagues who have supported my practice via referrals and otherwise including Denise, Kendall, Lisa, Barry, Mitch, Paul, Tony, Jen and Bob – I appreciate your trust and friendship.

CompassRose.com and Bookow.com – thank you for your editing services.

INTRODUCTION

I started working with and guiding the brand protection strategies of celebrities in the entertainment business in the late nineties. Back then, *"360 Record Deals,"* as they are commonly known, had just come to the fore and music artists were *forced* to develop a new appreciation for the ways that their names, likenesses and images (the essential elements of a "personal brand") are leveraged – often, by <u>others</u>. Everyone (creative, legal and business types alike) suddenly became much more "Brand-Cognizant." Fast forward 20 years - "brand" and "branding" are now the catchwords of the day; everything that anyone does – in *any* industry - is evaluated with an ear to the ground for "branding opportunities" in the near and distant future. We've all become a lot more aware of our ability to denote, convey, signify, harken and … influence.

Speaking of influence, social media is here to stay and, while it has its drawbacks, one thing is certain: in the context of brand development, promotion and marketing … social media *is* the "great equalizer." People with no ostensible talent or ability are now more well-known and influential than Olympic athletes, Nobel laureates, platinum artists, Oscar winners, NASA rocket scientists and the like. The good news is that, whether your "celebrity" was hard-won via creative/intellectual/business toil or the result of steadfast (round-the-clock) online networking, anyone (and everyone) now has the ability to create a successful brand. I can hear you, dear reader, saying "(i)s that ALWAYS such a good thing?" Again, the answer is yes. The ability to create a brand that promotes something useful for the betterment of society is always a good thing. To the extent that there are those who would use fame and notoriety in less desirable ways ... well, let's just hope that the words on the following pages are aspirational - "when they know better, they will do better."[1]

The reality is that no matter what line of business you're in, no matter your expertise or talent, if you enjoy any degree of celebrity and you aren't monetizing and using your name to sell a product or service of one kind or another, you are basically burning found money. Yup, just like going to the bank, clearing out your checking, savings and money-market accounts, dumping it all on the front lawn and lighting a match ala *Waiting to Exhale*. So, read on and take a page from the brand expansion playbooks of celebs like the "Jessicas" (Alba, Biel and Simpson) and others who have leveraged their fame to create industry-leading products (e.g., diapers, vodka/spirits, electronics, water, fashionable athleticwear, clothing, fragrances) and services (e.g., chicken and waffles/beer restaurants, fudge/popcorn shops, financial consulting, vegan drive-thrus).

But what should I *make, sell, serve?* That is for you to decide – based on what excites and motivates *you*. An analysis of trending markets is beyond the scope of this book; the goal here is simply to provide you with the information that you will need to **make meetings with your lawyers and business people meaningful and efficient**. I won't restate the disclaimer on the opening pages about this not being legal advice, etc. I *will* diverge for a moment to say this: if you are inspired to produce/sell a product or provide a service under a new brand and you take meetings in order to simply *receive* information, you're wasting everyone's time and a lot of your money. You should have a list of at least five questions to ask your lawyer, manager or marketing consultant about each of the topics that follow. A meeting is a mutual exchange of information. When a topic comes up and you have to say *"I hadn't thought about that,"* you've just put another check in someone's pocket – for the follow-up meeting, subsequent conference call, etc. I'm putting the schoolmarm glasses back in their case but please note the takeaway: BE PREPARED!

Clients sit across the table (or, more often, on the other end of the phone) and tell me, "I've got the ***p e r f e c t*** name … " pause. "Well, what have you got?" is my response. Seven out of ten times, it's a word or phrase that simply describes their product or service. (That's a bit of a "no-no" as we'll see in *Chapter 3 – Trademark Basics*.) But the other three times, I often hear something that is hands-down ingenious – evoking a smile or an audible laugh from me, an experienced marketing and trademark attorney who has seen it all – in consumer goods, retail services, pharmaceuticals, telecommunications, media … you name it; I've been on the front lines in support of some of the world's most brilliant ad-guys so it's really (*really*) hard to impress me.

But ... every now and then, someone presents an idea that's so clever and unexpected, I have to tip my hat and curtsy.

That said, having a fantastic name does not *automatically* result in a fantastic brand. There's a methodology that can buoy the most mediocre name choices. In the pages that follow, I summarize the "winning formula" that separates the successful brands from the super duds (the ones that swallow life savings in a single bound) using the five "Ps" -- ***PLANNING, PROTECTING, PROPER USE, POSITIONING, & POLICING.*** (Corny mnemonic? "Perhaps" but I bet you'll be "prepared" for any and all meetings about your brand from here on out.)

PLANNING: With a solid foundation built on awareness of who your customer is, where/how you plan to transact business and a vision of how and where your business is likely to expand in the future, you'll take the first step on the road to creating a reasonable brand protection plan.

PROTECTING. Make sure you assemble the appropriate people to register and enforce your intellectual property assets on your behalf.

PROPER USE: Once your portfolio is protected, you're in a position to launch an awesome marketing campaign and to display, share and otherwise attract attention. But ... all of your time and effort will be severely undermined if you're displaying the brand name improperly online, in promotional materials or elsewhere.

POSITIONING: For wealth-conscious readers, this is the section of the book that you'll probably want to skip ahead to. Don't. While it's understandable that you're eager to know more about reaping the rewards of your initial investment of time, creativity and money, your position in the negotiation of revenue generating agreements is infinitely better if your brand is properly protected. (That said, visions of strategic partnerships, sponsorships, merchandise licenses, retail distribution, franchises, etc. should totally motivate and inspire you ... to do the hard work upfront.)

POLICING. After all is said and done, you can spend a million dollars developing, marketing and leveraging your brand but it won't be worth a dime if you're not actively keeping an eye out for unauthorized users.

Helpful Tip. Before you begin, take a minute to glance at the *Glossary* and become familiar with unique terms that are frequently used in the context of brand protection/leveraging (and seldom used anywhere else).

.

[1] An indirect snippet of sage advice and wisdom bestowed by Maya Angelou and made famous by Oprah Winfrey.

PART I

PLANNING

CHAPTER 1

BRAND ELEMENTS

The combination of information, materials, visual elements, etc. that comprise your brand is as unique as your business and the personality/ideology that it represents. The following list is not exhaustive, by any means, however, at a minimum, these are points that you'll want to consider:

(A) Brand Fundamentals

Your brand is essentially a shorthand way of telling people who you are and what you represent – be it a particular lifestyle, characteristics, qualities, etc. It can be good or bad depending on those elements. It can consist of well-known or coveted knowledge depending on how extensively it is publicized and promoted. The parameters are limited only by your imagination and the scope of products/services you provide – now and in the future.

<u>*Your Business*</u>. Before discussing the elements that comprise your brand, take stock and identify your immediate business goals and the business you see yourself engaged in during the next five years. Here are a few examples:

- *You've designed a high-end line of clothing for pets, but you see yourself opening a pet-couture boutique within the next two years and, depending on how the boutique performs, selling franchises to others in another two years after that.*
- *If you currently make and deliver a smack-worthy open-faced sandwich to construction sites via food*

truck, but you have visions of a restaurant and/or a specialty artisan line of (carb-light, gluten-free) breads on the shelves of a national grocery chain.

- *Your immediate focus is the ideal post-workout meal replacement shake, but your five year plan includes water/shake bottles - perhaps a national line of fitness and/or wellness centers.*
- *As you're writing a brilliant screenplay, pay attention to your characters, their idiosyncrasies, style and the demographic that they represent.*

The takeaway: whatever you are doing right now is just a snapshot; force yourself to provide a bit of detail and color-in the *future* image of your business. Doing so will help you identify and embrace the timeless elements of your brand – now and for the future. (Subsequently making changes to a brand because you've outgrown it isn't just expensive; I've seen business people get stymied and lose momentum (and opportunities) when they have to stop and think of a new or variant brand name or logo.)

A Word About Social Media[2]. If you have a vibrant social media platform with a lot of traffic and connections, you have a potential customer base and clientele at the ready. Whether you have hundreds of followers on social media or millions doesn't matter; what matters is that the combination of photographs and narratives of and about you, your product or business have garnered attention and an audience of potential purchasers. If your primary livelihood is related to your new product/service line – great. As long as any contracts with your current employer/clients don't preclude it, you can probably use your existing platforms to introduce or segue into the new brand. However, if your day job is unrelated and/or if you have the aforementioned legal entanglements and obligations, your new brand should have its own social media portfolio – separate pages, accounts, contacts, etc.

Before leveraging a blog-following into a product/service line market, be careful about oversharing and about the "way" that you refer to your product/service. Perhaps because the nature of a blog is to share and generate personal or semi-personal information, this is harder to avoid than it sounds. Instructions regarding the use and presentation of your trademarks and other brand elements online and in print are set forth in *Chapters 7* and *10*. Study them.

Optimize each platform and tailor it for your business needs. After your website, *FaceBook* is the first place that customers and competitors look for important information about your business; use it to share updates, commentary about current trends and to respond to customers. *Twitter* is crucial for the exchange of customer-driving information in 140 characters or less. *Pinterest* and *Instagram* are essential when conveying visual representations of your products and services. (We'll discuss logos in the next section but keep in mind that the dimensions of your logo have to be appropriate and appealing when viewed on a variety of platforms and devices.) If you are a brick-and-mortar operation that is location driven, up-to-date profiles and immediate responses to reviews on *Yelp* and *FourSquare* are required. Relationships between suppliers, vendors and potential employees are fostered most effectively using *LinkedIn*.

Brand Names. The core of your brand will obviously be the way that you refer to your business, product or service – your brand-name which, when properly used and protected, becomes your "trademark."

Terms: *"Trademark," "mark," "brand," "brand name," "name," are often used interchangeably. Most attorneys use "trademark" and "mark" to refer specifically to words, symbols and anything else that can qualify for registration in the United States Patent and Trademark Office. A "name" or "brand name" is simply a word or phrase that you use as the name of a business, product or service. The term "brand" is all-encompassing and, at the time of this writing, rather fluid. When properly used, it can be thought of as the sensory depiction and perception of your product/company persona.*

The process for protecting a trademark is summarized in *Chapter 3*. At this point, if you don't already have a word or phrase in mind for your brand name, complete the exercises in the next and last sections of this chapter which provide guidance on the selection of logos (the visual symbols that represent your brand). (Even if you don't want to use a symbol (yet), note that it's often easier to *visualize* the characteristics that you want to convey via your brand; the logo creation tools that I've provided may help you get there.)

In all cases, you want to balance the very practical need to communicate and suggest information, on the one hand, against the desire to be clever, unique and memorable, on the other hand. Your name should do much more than simply describe your product or service. But at the same time, you don't want a name that is so obscure and random that no one has any idea about what the heck you're selling. The exception would be where you have a bottomless, unlimited advertising and promotions budget (e.g., "*Apple*" for computers); with *that,* you can basically teach and train the public to associate your brand name (no matter how random) with your product and your product alone.

Images. Make sure that any photographs, drawings, pictures, or other graphic/visual elements that you incorporate in your logo, website and marketing materials are yours or obtain permission to use them. Images and photographs are protected by copyright law so, unless you've completed the process outlined in *Chapter 4,* you are leaving yourself exposed to potential liability if you don't own these materials outright and/or if you haven't obtained an express consent and approval to use them – ideally, without any limitations.

Other Intellectual Property. As we'll see in *Chapter 3,* almost anything can function as a trademark (e.g., words, colors, designs – even scents and sounds). But you should also look at your products and your place of business – what is unique about, e.g., the appearance of your products and packaging, the décor of your store or establishment, the design of your website, an app that you've created - as compared to your competitors?

Example: *Consider the seafood restauranteur who, though eager to jump on the living-wall trend in restaurant décor, artfully displays a vertical, floor to ceiling mushroom patch (instead of the more popular green vegetation) on a reclaimed ship hull at the entrance of each of his restaurants.*

In addition to trademarks and copyrights, elements of your brand may also be covered by other areas of *intellectual property* – for example, the inventions (tools, processes, even mobile applications) and designs you've created may very well qualify for protection via utility patents, design patents or trade dress.

Example: *Picture the fashion designer who, tired of holding bulky fabric as she's sewing and, out of desperation, configures a hook, pipe cleaner, roll of pennies and two fingers from a latex glove into an apparatus that suspends the fabric with just the right amount of tension as it enters the machine feeder and sewing needle.*

The basic tests for patentability are outlined in *Chapter 4* but, suffice it to say that in compiling the elements of your brand, in addition to cute slogans, you should be thinking about the totality of your contribution to your industry in the context of your enterprise. (A good intellectual property attorney will help you spot potential proprietary assets and gaps in protection. They should also provide you with a cost vs. benefits overview so you can decide whether it's worth it to seek protection of your rights – now, or later, as your brand develops.)

(B) LOGOS AND OTHER VISUAL BRAND ELEMENTS

Some Famous Logos. A *white apple silhouette with a single bite missing. Golden arches.* A *red circle inside another red circle.* Without even seeing the pictorial representation, you read the above descriptions and instantly know that I'm referring to the following famous brands: *Apple, McDonald's, Target.* That's the beauty of a logo – if a picture is worth a 1,000 words, a logo is worth 1,000,000. It communicates your most important message to your customer/client in a single glance.

Apple's white, bitten apple communicates clean, cutting edge functionality and usefulness. (The bite-mark and the color also serve to distinguish it from the Beatle's round green apple logo – the subject of 30 years of litigation.)[3] *Target's* bullseye tells you that you've come the right place for anything and everything – from winter coats to bookshelves to avocados. *McDonald's* golden arches? They are said to mirror the design of the original *McDonald's* structures but the only visual that comes to mind are two quasi-addictive, shoe-string French-fries found at the bottom of a *McDonald's* bag. Bingo – mission accomplished; the owners of these brands have all guided would-be customers into thinking about their products and devices – just by picturing their logos.

Types of Logos. There are essentially three broad categories that most logos will fall into: (a) *Stylized Typography* (picture the *Gucci, Prada, Exxon* logos), (b) *Combined Typography* and *Graphics Elements* (think about the *Bonefish Grill* sign and the fish skeleton between those two words), and (c) *Graphic Pictorial* (revisit *Apple's* bitten white apple). What kind will you use? The answer should depend entirely on the message you want to convey to would-be customers.

Distilling the Essence of Your Message. You have to be able to describe your target customer and the ways that your particular product/service fulfills a need in their lives. By the time you purchase a book like this, that should sound relatively easy. The real challenge is to tap and identify the *emotion* associated with the customer's need and … the fulfillment of it. (If the preceding sentence seems a little racy – welcome to the world of advertising and marketing; you will be appealing to the sentient nature of sentient beings. Accept that and move on or pick up a psychology of advertising book.)

What is special about your product/services when you look around at what your competitors are doing (or not doing)? How does that special quality *feel*? These are questions that you MUST answer for yourself before you spend one red cent with a graphic artist.

The other thing that you should do (before someone else does) is consider all the bad jokes that might be made about the logo in the context of your line of business. By way of example, if the brand you envision connotes exclusivity and luxury, having a pictorial representation that resembles a penny is not going to be a good look for you. To the contrary, if you are planning to parody something that is already a part of the common vernacular and lexicon of your industry (cautiously – see

Chapter 11), you may indeed want to poke fun at your business and your brand.

(C) CHARACTERS & SIGNATURE PRODUCT LINES

Marketable Characters. If you've written a screenplay or a pilot for a television series, before your work is sold, review it for marketable characters and features that can be licensed to third-party manufacturers. Programs that are targeted to children are renowned for their ability to generate huge sums from toy, game, and costume manufacturers. Fully one third or seven billion dollars of the 21 billion dollars in revenue generated by the *Harry Potter* series was earned in connection with merchandise.[4] Other series like *Batman* and *Star Wars*, animated films/programs such as *Frozen, Sponge Bob* and shows like the *Game of Thrones* boast similar revenue proportions generated by the sale of character-centered merchandise.

Example: *A treatment for an episodic television program appealing to tweens is currently being reviewed and evaluated. The protagonist is a teenage girl signed to a record deal whose hair is a different color each week. In addition to apparel, temporary hair color cosmetics and home-recording audio-visual equipment might also represent potential sources of merchandise income.*

The name and (separately) the pictorial representation of each such character should be registered as a trademark.

Signature Products. Character-related merchandise is

primarily targeted to children. (There are some exceptions – e.g., the *50 Shades of Grey Teddy Bears* discussed in *Chapter 12* and the adults who still purchase *Hello Kitty* and *Batman* products.) Businesses that target all demographics can identify multiple products that are natural extensions of the brand owner's primary product or service line.

Example: *A combination wine /cigar bar opens for business. In addition to signature wines and cigars, the owner also anticipates that patrons will purchase corkscrews, cigar cutters, wine racks, desk humidors and other small accessories. Although wine refrigerators are beyond the owner's expertise and production capability, he has the foresight to anticipate a license arrangement with a refrigeration manufacture so … he wisely includes "refrigeration" in the scope of business that he intends to claim in the future via an intent-to-use ("ITU") application, discussed in* Chapter 3.

	Chapter 1 Take-Away Notes:
1.	***Your brand's one sentence elevator message:***
2.	***Description of your customer (where they shop,***
	where they work, what they do on the
	weekend):
3.	***List the probable sentiments that motivate***
	a purchase of your product/service:
4.	***List the colors and shapes that address***
	the sentiments in 3 above (e.g., vanity, worry,
	frugality, health-consciousness, indulgence,
	necessity/survival, elitism, discomfort, etc.):

[2]Entire books have been written about the critical role that social media plays in marketing and brand development. Among them, see *SOCIAL MEDIA MARKETING; A STRATEGIC APPROACH* 2ND ED., Melissa Barker (2017 Cengage Learning).

[3] Alex, Salkever, *John, Paul, George, Ringo ... and Steve?*, BLOOMBERG BUSINESSWEEK, September 30, 2004

[4] Madeleine Kruhly, *Harry Potter, Inc.: How the Boy Wizard Created a $21 Billion Business*, THE ATLANTIC, July 15, 2011

CHAPTER 2

YOUR BRAND TEAM

Trademark Attorney. This is obvious. There are some lawyers who prepare trademark applications and do other things as well – e.g., litigate divorce cases, represent you in a real estate purchase, help you settle an insurance claim, etc. That's completely fine – the basics of filing a trademark application are fairly straightforward and you can use a general practice attorney for that purpose. The caveat is that the process can become complicated later on and you'll have to live with whatever is done at the start. A useful analogy is the comparison of a general dentist and an endodontist (a root canal specialist); the general dentist can do a filling and some may even do a basic, run-of-the-mill root canal but if it gets complicated or (worse) if there's a complication that isn't detected from the start … ?

Specific steps in the trademark process are discussed more extensively in *Chapter 3* but the bottom line is this: if the person representing you in the United States Patent & Trademark Office (also known as the "USPTO," "PTO" or "Trademark (Patent) Office") is not knowledgeable about trademark law and/or is not clever in terms of appreciating marketing concepts and the use of words, find someone else. A trademark lawyer *must* be able to understand the intersection of nuanced market segments as well as the intended meaning/significance of a word and its context. (If you get a blank stare or a *"let me think about it and get back to you"* when you mention a modification or witty twist, move on.) This person is often (but not always) someone who is singularly focused on trademark prosecution in the USPTO and TTAB, brand licensing, enforcement against trademark infringers, etc. Choose your representative carefully – make sure that they spend time with you outlining the process and answering all of your questions. They are not going to conduct an all-out search for you for free or make any guarantees regarding an outcome but they should take the time to walk you through the process – what can happen, when, how long, options, approximate costs, etc.

General Practice Attorney. If you go the route of hiring a trademark expert, you can expect them to represent you in the USPTO, in contentious proceedings (e.g., infringement litigation if that's a part of your engagement/retention arrangement) and in negotiations of licenses, distribution agreements and other agreements wherein you will leverage your brand. There are things that they will not do for you – e.g., the aforementioned real estate closings, divorce proceedings, etc. That's just not what they do. Indeed, because so much of a trademark lawyer's practice is based on referrals from general practice attorneys, they often avoid other unrelated areas of practice - not because of any actual conflict of interests or because they are incapable but because maintaining a clear line of demarcation in practice areas is better for business. (To use the dental analogy again: if the orthodontist who put braces on your kids' teeth also offered to start doing *your* fillings and tooth cleanings, how long do you think your general dentist will continue to refer business to him?)

Graphic Artist. Even if you don't have a logo design in mind, it's a good idea to play with a few concepts and remain open to inspiration – whatever the source. We live in a visual, multi-lingual society, with porous virtual borders; a good graphic artist can work with you to design a pictorial element of your mark that will positively impact your brand – whether it's viewed from afar on a billboard in Beijing or up close on a mobile device on a plane.

Web Designer. This might be the same person as your graphic artist but not always. The main things to consider when engaging your web designer (assuming that your website is not a DIY project) are: (a) your specifications for content and functionality and (b) a written understanding of pricing for creation, revisions, updates, and maintenance.

Marketing Guru. If you are reading this book, there's a good chance that you may be planning to define and guide your own brand marketing strategy. If you have a choice, don't do it. You know what they say about the lawyer who represents his or herself? He/she has a fool for a client. The same is true for high-stakes, big budget marketing. When you are emotionally invested in a creative endeavor – like creating a brand - you simply don't have the necessary objectivity to edit, hire/fire, discard, slash, and burn. I know exactly what you're thinking: "I've met plenty of marketing professionals and if THEY can do it ...?" You're right, there are plenty of "de facto" marketing folks who have the gift of gab and spend all of their waking hours networking (partying). I'm not talking about them. I'm talking about the *brilliant* people who know exactly how to identify and reach

YOUR target market. They know which colors to use, what type of social media will be most effective, how to stretch a brand introduction budget until it hollers, etc. How do you identify them? Look around at brands that are popular within your intended demographic.

Other Professionals. If you're already at the point where you want to franchise your business, seek out a lawyer who has extensive experience in franchise law. There are some aspects of business that are expensive to correct and redo; an improperly created franchise can ruin your business and your brand. Moreover, if your business is heavily regulated (e.g., medical/spa services, finance, etc.) compliance with applicable federal, state and local laws will be a critical factor – for all matters, including the display and content of your brand and whether/how you are even permitted to offer franchises and enter licenses. Sometimes marketing/trademark attorneys have regulatory compliance experience because of the physical proximity of label/disclosure issues and intellectual property; when in doubt, ask. It goes without saying that, if you're in any kind of business, you should have an accountant/tax person on speed dial.

General Remarks About Working as a Team. Designing a brand that reflects your ideology and vision is a collaborative effort; chose team-members who will work well with other professionals and make your brand identity a priority. That sounds elementary but, when your graphic artist refuses to make a revision necessitated by a conversation with your trademark attorney or if you can't reach your trademark attorney for an approval of a revised drawing prior to your launch deadline, these words will echo in your ears.

Scouting. Get recommendations from colleagues you respect. Online reviews are easy to fake or influence with the payment of subscriptions, etc. If a recommendation is not available, ask to see examples of the professional's work and/or to speak with former clients. In terms of identifying and evaluating a brand/trademark specialist, if you are technically savvy, go online at USPTO.gov, do a search[5] for the attorney's name and open the files for which he/she is listed as the *"Attorney of Record."* USPTO files are part of the public record so you can actually open documents like *Responses to Office Actions*. Check to make sure that the name of the attorney is on the documents that were actually filed and trace the outcome – did the application actually result in a registration? Did the *Attorney of Record* actually outsource the matter to another lawyer, paralegal or third-party company?

	Chapter 2 Take-Away Notes:
1.	***Budget for legal? (Fees vary widely for service***
	providers ranging from online to large firms.)
2.	***Budget for graphics?***
3.	***Budget for website?***
4.	***Names of recommended professionals?***

[5] The USPTO *Trademark Assistance Center* number is (800) 786-9199.

PART II

PROTECTING

CHAPTER 3

TRADEMARK BASICS

(A) GENERAL OVERVIEW

When discussing the subject of brand protection, several areas of *Intellectual Property* and *Commercial Law* are implicated – they include *Copyrights, Patents, Trade Secrets, Rights of Privacy, Unfair Competition,* etc. However, by far, the legal discipline that predominates when a brand of any value is at issue is *Trademark Law.* It's a deceptively simple area of the law: you come up with a name, you claim it as your own and nobody else can use it – right? Not quite. This field is a landmine wrapped in a trick-bag for the novice as well as the veteran entrepreneur. It is always (and in all ways) advisable to seek professional help before venturing down this road. Below, I've arranged some of the key topics you'll want to be familiar with before your first meetings. (This is "heady" stuff; you don't want to encounter it for the first time while you're evaluating what's right/wrong for your particular brand. So, think of it as "prep-work".)

When discussing the subject of brand protection, the legal discipline that predominates is trademark law.

What is a trademark (or a "mark")? A trademark is almost anything (typically a word, phrase or symbol but sometimes a sound, style or even a smell) that tells the world that your product/service comes from ... you. When you obtain protection in a trademark, you can prevent others from using it in a way that is *"likely to cause confusion"* with your business.

What a trademark is not. A trademark does NOT protect

original works of authorship like a book, sound recording, film, ad copy or film treatment – those things are covered by *copyright law* (covered in *Chapter 4*). A trademark does NOT protect novel/useful inventions and processes like a mobile app., exercise equipment device, or a cosmetic concealer that functions as a pigment lightener and sun protectant – those things are covered by *patent law* (also discussed in *Chapter 4*).

How does a brand element (e.g., a name) become a protected trademark? From the time that you start using your word/phrase/design as a trademark, you have what are called *"common law"* rights as a trademark owner under the LANHAM ACT.[6] So, even if you never attempt to register it, once you use it, you have common law rights that you can use to enforce your rights - *albeit,* in a limited manner. The references to "use" are critical and rather specific – as you'll see in a moment. (That's why they're underlined!)

Symbols. *A shortcut for determining whether or not a mark is registered is the little **TM** (for trademarks claimed in connection with products) or **SM** (for service marks claimed in connection with services) that you see next to some brand-names. If there's no ®, the mark has not obtained registration. If there's a **TM** or **SM**, someone has probably applied for registration. (At the very least, you know that anyone using **TM** or **SM** is aware of his or her rights and is claiming the exclusive right to use it with certain products/services; they have put the world "on notice" of their claim.)*

Why register a trademark? The main reason that people

register their marks is because it can be very difficult to enforce a mark that is not registered. By registering your mark in the USPTO, in addition to gaining a "presumption of ownership," you also gain the ability to bring an infringement action in federal court – an obvious advantage if the alleged infringer is in, e.g., Portland and you're in Philadelphia. As if that wasn't incentive enough, please be advised that media networks like *FaceBook, Youtube* and *Twitter* will typically ask you to provide a valid registration number if you ever want to report and seek removal of unauthorized uses of a mark that is similar to yours.

There are other advantages. For one thing, if (when!) you're presented with a lucrative licensing, distribution or venture capitalization offer, you are in a stronger position if your mark is already registered and you can attach, e.g., a schedule of domestic and international registrations to your agreement. Your registration also has deterrent value; it will be found in searches by the USPTO and by other businesses/individuals when they consider whether or not the mark is already in use. Yet another reason to register is that trademark registrants can take advantage of certain border and international protections and treaties that curtail the creation of counterfeit goods abroad and the importation of them back into the U.S.

Should you register the words, the logos (pictures/designs) or both? While trademark law can protect the pictorial (design) elements of your brand (e.g., Target's red dot in a circle or *Gucci's* interwoven "Gs"), it is not always necessary or feasible to do so. If your budget is unlimited and you have an actual graphic design (something more than a pre-loaded and ubiquitous font), sure, why not – in Intellectual Property land, there's nothing wrong with a belt, suspenders *and* a bow tie. But, if your budget is limited or if your design doesn't add anything unique or special to your brand, you should ask yourself this question: how will you feel if you see someone using the "design" (e.g., a small blue line over a green triangle) in connection with a word or phrase that is completely different from the words/phrases that comprise your brand?

If you can shrug it off, you will probably sleep comfortably knowing that you've saved some money and you don't care if you see that line and triangle all over town and the Internet. On the other hand, if the blue is a *special* blue and the triangle symbolizes the bond amongst you and your business partners, etc., go ahead and invest in a separate application for the registration of your logo.

You *could* file what is known as a combined ("composite") word/logo mark but I don't usually recommend it unless you fall in love with the logo and your budget can't accommodate two applications. Why? Well, you know what they say about a "jack of all trades" being the "master of none"? That's sort of how I feel about combined word/logo marks – there's a school of thought that says that, when an application combines word elements and a logo, each of those elements loses some of its breadth and reach.

Example. *Please take a look at the illustration (on the next page) and the table on the page after that as you consider the following example: The name of Sue's restaurant (in the middle of the desert, where there isn't a flower in sight) is PETALS'.*

*Sue, who has always been a dog lover, decided long ago to use an old image of her favorite dog as a puppy with a pink collar in her logo design (**Figure 3.1**). A customer walks in one day and tells her that a new restaurant just opened down the road and they are calling their place PETAL VIEW … but (in an effort to make Sue feel better) he adds that these other folks are using a covered bridge as the logo on their sign, their menu and all their advertisements (**Figure 3.2**).*

*Sue takes out her tablet to assess the situation and while Googling, what does she see? A pop-up ad for yet another new restaurant about a mile down the road in the other direction! These other folks are calling their place RUCKUS ROADSIDE but, would you believe it, the logo on their website and at the entrance to their place is … a puppy with a pink collar design! (**Figure 3.3**.) What is Sue to do?*

FIGURE 3.1 (Sue's trademark)

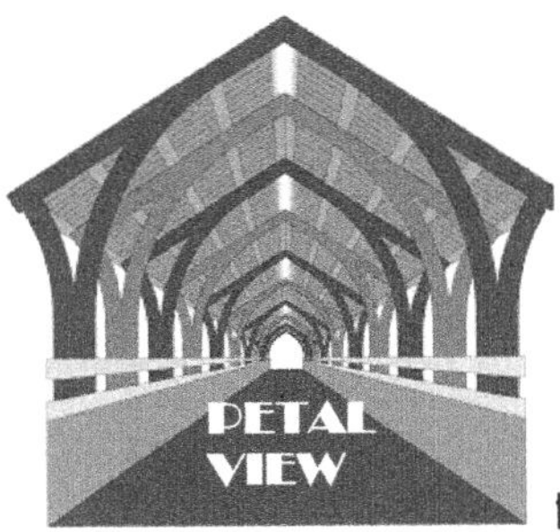

FIGURE 3.2 (Competitor A)

Figure 3.3 (Competitor B)

TABLE 3.1 – SUE'S PROTECTION STRATEGY ANALYZED

TYPE OF TRADEMARK APPLICATION /REGISTRATION:	WHAT IT'S CAPABLE OF COVERING:	SUE'S CLAIM OF EXCLUSIVE RIGHTS IN THE RESTAURANT BUSINESS:	HOW WILL THIS TYPE OF REGISTRATION HELP SUE?
WORD MARK	Words and phrases in any form, any style, font or context.	The use of the word PETALS – in any form, style, color, etc.	Enables her to challenge *Competitor A (Figure 3.2)* because the word "PETAL" is the dominant portion of both marks.
LOGO (DESIGN) MARK	A particular pictorial, graphic or artistic representation, style or image.	Labrador-looking dog images in black & white outline form. Dogs wearing collars that display a word/phrase. The prominent use of the color pink. The combination of these elements.	Enables her to challenge *Competitor B (Figure 3.3)* based on similarity of the design features that are common to both.
COMPOSITE (COMBO) WORD/LOGO MARK	The word and the design elements of a mark.	Covers the word PETALS as used in connection with the dog design.	It will provide her with *some* protection against both competitors. However, protection is not as comprehensive as it would be if she obtained the separate word registration AND logo registration described above. vs. Competitor A: The additional wording ("VIEW") and the obvious distinctions between a *covered bridge* vs. a *dog* will be used by *Competitor A* to argue that confusion is not likely. vs. Competitor B: The fact that the names (PETALS vs. RUCKUS ROADHOUSE) are lacking in similarity in terms of meaning, appearance and sound will be used by *Competitor B* (along with their dog's purple lightning bolt tattoo) to argue that confusion is not likely.

What is the registration process? Essentially, trademark registration involves a two-step process: (i) *clearance* and (ii) the prosecution of an *application* in the USPTO. Simple? Sometimes. Nuanced? Always.

(B) STEP ONE OF THE TRADEMARK REGISTRATION PROCESS: "CLEARING" OR "SEARCHING" THE MARK.

During the *clearance* or *"search"* process, a trademark attorney will engage a third party data collection firm (a "search company") to compile and review current applications and registrations for marks that are identical or closely similar to your mark. In order to meet prevailing standards of due diligence, the review will also identify businesses and individuals who may have acquired *"common law"* trademark rights (described above) simply by using the mark.

Due Diligence Opinion Letters & What's Protectable. Depending on what is revealed in the search, your trademark attorney will write an opinion (also known as an *"Opinion Letter"*) regarding your ability to use the mark in one or more areas of commerce. See the example in *Appendix 3A*.

Even before the search is ordered, I try to provide clients with an assessment of whether or not a mark is even "protectable" (i.e., capable of being registered as a trademark). (For example, if it merely describes a product or a generic feature, registration will either be refused outright or postponed until you are able to present evidence of consumer recognition of your trademark/product connection.)

<u>Protectability</u>. There's a spectrum of classifications (see *Table 3.2* below) starting with the easiest to register – *arbitrary* or *fanciful* marks.

Table 3.2 Spectrum of Protectability

Type	Practical Meaning	Examples
Fanciful	Coined or "made-up" word that has no other meaning	*Google, Exxon, Polaroid, Starbucks*
Arbitrary	A real word but it has no apparent connection to the product or service.	*Apple, Shell, Brother*
Suggestive	Hints at a feature or attribute of a product or service.	*Friendly's, Boost, Big Lots, Bonefish Grill*
Descriptive	Describes a feature or attribute of a product or service.	*SportsCream, OfficeDepot, Home Goods*
Generic	Word is now the primary way that the market refers to the product or service.	*Aspirin, Escalator, Cellophane, App, Thermos, Yo-Yo*

I absolutely <u>love</u> marks in these first two categories; they make my job *so* simple. Think of the completely *arbitrary* (i.e., random) nature of the *APPLE* mark in the context of computers and the *fanciful EXXON* mark which, to my knowledge has no meaning whatsoever in the English language – that's the very definition of "fanciful" in trademark parlance.

Occupying the next rung on the ladder of protectability are marks that are *suggestive*. Think of the *BONEFISH GRILL* mark and the way that it *suggests* or "hints" at the idea of a seafood dinner. Suggestive marks are not as easily protected as arbitrary or fanciful marks because, often, the Trademark Office will initially relegate them to the next category, *descriptive* marks, which are *not* protectable unless you have actual evidence that customers associate the mark with you and your business. An example of a descriptive mark might be *LA FITNESS*. Unless and until that brand became famous, a reference to *LA FITNESS* could have just as easily been the way that any and all fitness centers in Los Angeles *describe* their businesses.

#Hashtags. *While the USPTO does accept applications to register a word or phrase as a hashtag, unless it represents a name or product that is already well known, an application for a hashtag mark will probably receive a descriptiveness refusal on grounds that it merely describes a topic or group of posts/comments on social media.*

Last on the list and the one you want to avoid at all costs is the *generic* term – notice I didn't use the word "mark" because, unlike all of the other categories, a generic term is not even *capable* of becoming a trademark - ever. It's so commonly used that it is now the primary way to refer to a product or service. The term ESCALATOR was once a trademark but because you now use that term instead of, e.g., "moving staircase" to refer to a mode of travel from one floor to the next, it lost its status as a trademark. In *Chapter 10*, the ways to use your mark in order to prevent it from becoming generic are outlined.

Value of the Opinion Letter. As shown in ***Appendix 3A***, an *Opinion Letter* goes into great detail regarding the existence of marks that might or might not be similar to yours. It's a good thing to have in your file in case you are ever sued by someone claiming senior rights in your mark. You can point to it and say *"see, I did my due diligence and acted in good faith; I certainly didn't* intend *to infringe your mark."*

Scope of Search – Get a Lay of the Land re Areas of Expansion. Depending on the type of search you request (limited or broad, focused on one area of business or inclusive of multiple areas), the *Opinion Letter* is also a great way to identify which areas of expansion may be open to you (e.g., in *Chapter 1,* the example we provided was a chain of fitness centers that started out as a protein drink). A benefit of requesting a search and Opinion Letter (and incurring the expense that it requires) is that you avoid (or at least anticipate) "substantive" refusals based on likelihood of confusion with a prior registration (or earlier filed application) which can, on occasion, render you dead-in-the-water

Risks Associated with Not Searching. There are times when people will skip or waive the search and simply proceed to the application. That's obviously not ideal so, if you are presented with this option, weigh it carefully and do an actual cost (they are expensive) versus benefits analysis. If you can afford it, get it; if not, know that you are accepting the risks associated with not searching ahead of time.

Heads-Up: *Not searching/clearing a mark means you may have to pay your attorney to respond to an Office Action if the USPTO cites a prior-filed registration or application against yours. The worst case scenario is when neither you nor the USPTO find out about someone else who is already using the mark. When this happens after you've invested substantial sums in registering and promoting your brand, it can be very costly – especially if you end up having to defend against allegations of trademark infringement.*

(C) STEP TWO OF THE TRADEMARK REGISTRATION PROCESS: FILING AN APPLICATION FOR REGISTRATION

The "claim" or "identification." In the same way that the search is specific areas of industry, the application is filed in designated "classes." Why not file in all classes, for everything? Because each class requires payment of a separate fee that ranges from between $225 and $400 depending on the mode of filing (restricted, digital, or paper) that you use. A list of available classifications is set forth in *Appendix 3B*.

The "drawing" for logo or design marks. If you are claiming a mark that contains anything more than standard lettering, you will have to submit a "drawing" of the exact depiction of your mark – including references to color if color is a feature of your mark (e.g., the way that the color red dominates *Target's* dot in a circle logo).

The "use" requirement. The concept of "use" in the context of trademarks in the United States is key; you will NOT get a registration unless and until you are able to show (through submission of actual evidence/specimens) that you are using the mark in international or interstate commerce. Even though it is possible to file an application based simply on your *intention-to-use* a mark in the future, you will not receive a *Certificate of Trademark Registration* until your evidence of use is accepted by the USPTO.

Use on Goods. In the context of retail and consumer goods, this generally means submission of hang-tags, labels and packaging materials wherein the mark is displayed. When your "store" is your website, it means that the mark must be positioned very specifically in relation to your products – in terms of size, prominence, order placement information, etc. (Issues specific to online stores are covered in *Chapter 7.)*

Use in connection with Services. The evaluation of specimens that are submitted in connection with services hinges on whether or not the services are described in reasonable proximity to the mark. The typical example is a brochure (or the digital equivalent, discussed in *Chapter 7*). Other acceptable specimens include letterhead (as long as the services are described somewhere in the letterhead header/footer or in the body of an actual letter) and advertising (where the message is direct and not abstract).

The Examination Process. Several months after filing, the USPTO will (ideally) approve your application for "publication" (a 30 day period during which other people can object to your application on grounds that your mark is likely to cause confusion with theirs). If it is not approved, the USPTO will issue an *Office Action* that requires a response. As explained below, the subject of an *Office Action* can range from the mundane (the drawing of your logo isn't clear) to intense (the mark merely *describes* your products or is *likely to cause confusion* with someone else's mark). If you ever receive an *Office Action* or any other correspondence from the USPTO, it is always advisable to consult an attorney – even if you think the matter is simple and that you can handle it yourself. (You don't want to say or do something that can and will come back to bite you later. The USPTO has an intricate set of rules and requirements that can take *years* to learn how to navigate efficiently; if this is your first rodeo – and even if it's your 10th – go find a seat up in the stands and leave the Office Actions to the pros.)

Office Action Subject Matter. Please refer to *Table 3.3* below which outlines the primary categories of refusals that the USPTO can use to block registration. Attorneys who have "prosecuted" several applications in the USPTO are generally aware of how to respond to each of the primary types of refusals and how they prepare persuasive arguments in a *Response to Office Action* or a *Request for Reconsideration* (the last step before filing an appeal). These responses require research and careful analysis of relevant case law in the context of the USPTO's particular basis for refusal. An example is provided in the excerpt in *Appendix 3C*.

TABLE 3.3 – COMMON REFUSALS IN USPTO TRADEMARK OFFICE ACTIONS

<table>
<tr><th colspan="2">SUBSTANTIVE REFUSALS</th></tr>
<tr><th>TYPE</th><th>DESCRIPTION</th></tr>
<tr><td>DESCRIPTIVENESS</td><td>• A word or design mark merely describes the goods/services that the Applicant is selling.
• Often includes a request that the Applicant "disclaim" a portion of the mark. (Means that the Applicant does not claim an exclusive right to use the word – separately.)
• A showing of secondary meaning will be required if the refusal is not withdrawn or won on appeal.</td></tr>
<tr><td>LIKELIHOOD OF CONFUSION ("LOC")</td><td>• Someone else has already filed an application and/or obtained a registration for a similar mark in connection with similar goods/services.
• Can be overcome but it's difficult and costly; that's why you try to identify whatever the USPTO might "cite" against you during the Search/Clearance process.</td></tr>
<tr><td>ORNAMENTATION</td><td>• The mark is not being used as a trademark but is instead being used as a decoration on, e.g., a shirt.
• Again, for marks that are used in connection with goods/products, the preferred manner of use is on a label, tag, packaging or, if online, on a screen where the product is displayed and where consumers can click to order.</td></tr>
<tr><td>FUNCTIONALITY</td><td>• Features claimed as trade dress are actually essential or practical for the use of the item.</td></tr>
<tr><td>SCANDALOUS MATTERS</td><td>• A mark contains a word, phrase or picture that most people would find offensive on its face.</td></tr>
<tr><th colspan="2">REFUSALS BASED ON FORMALITIES</th></tr>
<tr><td>IDENTIFICATION OF GOODS</td><td>• The list of claimed goods/services is indefinite and requires clarification in terms of wording.
• The list includes goods/services that fall under additional categories and therefore require payment of additional fees.</td></tr>
<tr><td>DRAWING</td><td>• Lacks clarity and/or does not conform to the USPTO's technical requirements.</td></tr>
<tr><td>SPECIMENS OF USE</td><td>• Doesn't show the mark used in a true trademark sense.
• Doesn't match the drawing submitted with the application.</td></tr>
</table>

The two most frequent bases for substantive refusal, as noted above, are *Descriptiveness* and *Likelihood of Confusion*. If you have an apparel brand, there's a good chance that you will encounter an *Ornamentation* refusal and if you're seeking to protect the design of a product or its packaging (see the discussion of *Trade Dress* in *Chapters 4* and *5*), your application may have to endure *Functionality* scrutiny.

Appeals. If the Examiner assigned to your application does not accept arguments that are made in support of your application, you and your lawyer can file an *Ex Parte Appeal* in the *Trademark Trial and Appeal Board* (the "TTAB").

Oppositions. During the 30 day publication period mentioned above, if someone objects to your right to register your mark, they will file a *Notice of Opposition* (if they are deciding whether/not to oppose your application, they will request an extension of that 30 day deadline). These are gnarly, potentially "end-of-the-road" matters (discussed in greater detail in *Chapter 18)*. The main take-away is that you want to avoid this situation by identifying and eliminating marks that might be opposed early on – during the due diligence, *Search/Clearance* phase. Note that even if you ultimately prevail in an opposition challenge, you still have to incur the (substantial) cost of defending your application and your right to use and register your mark.

Registration. If all goes well and your application is approved without opposition and/or if you prevail in an actual *Opposition Proceeding,* you will be approved for registration and a *Certificate of Registration* will be sent to you. Please refer to *Chapter 17* for tips on maintaining your registration.

Fees. It isn't cheap. (Whoever gives you a quote for services should spend enough time explaining what is included versus what is excluded to make you feel comfortable. If they get an attitude when you ask for a breakdown in writing ... ?) There are online trademark registration services that can be less expensive, initially, than consulting a traditional law firm. Before you hit "order," be sure you understand exactly what's included in the online fee and what may later require additional payment if and when, e.g., an Office Action is received that has to be referred to … a traditional law firm.

	Chapter 3 Take-Away Notes:
1.	***What can function as a trademark?***
2.	***Why should you register the trademark elements of your brand?***
3.	***Can you register a trademark before you start using it?***
4.	***What are the risks associated with not conducting a trademark search?***
5.	***What can you use as evidence of use of your products/services?***

---

[6] 15 U.S.C. Section 1051 et. seq.

CHAPTER 4

Other Intellectual Property Assets

(A) GENERAL OVERVIEW

The other reason you and your general practice attorney may call in a trademark expert is because they are usually well-versed in other areas of intellectual property ("IP") and can spot issues, potential problems and opportunities that center around IP assets that you may not even be aware of. For example, if you've created a mobile app, depending on its purpose, you may be able to obtain a utility patent in its functionality. Similarly, if you've designed an article of clothing that has a unique design, you may be able to use a *design patent* to protect elements of the design that are not dictated by function (translation: they don't fasten, suspend, secure an article/garment or otherwise serve a functional purpose). There is often overlap between what constitutes *Trade Dress* (a subset of trademarks discussed in *Chapters 5 and 8*) and what constitutes a design that can be protected by copyright and/or patent law. For good measure, let's also throw in the fact that the content (pictures, text copy and overall layout and feel) of your website is probably copyrightable and that, if you engage e.g., vendors or other contractors to help you manufacturer and market your products, you may have to disclose proprietary information (i.e., *trade secrets* like recipes, processes, collected data) that you don't want to share with the world.

Herein lies the rub: some of these elements compete with each other. For example, when you publish (or "make public") elements of, e.g., your trade dress or your copyrightable materials, you start the clock running in the patent department. Similarly, if you extol the functional qualities (e.g., *"the gizmo-glasses serve three distinct purposes – visual enhancement, minimization of crow's feet and improved outlook"*) on your website, you are not going to be able to use your website to support protection of your trade dress and design patent applications – both of which can be refused if your item is deemed to be "functional."

So, the take-away is: get a complete lay of the IP landscape (including the cliff around the bend and the quicksand on the other side of the hill) ... *before* you leap.

(B) Patents

Patent Basics. An invention is potentially protectable as a United States patent if it meets three requirements: (1) it has to be *useful*, (2) it has to have *novel* features and (3) it *can't be an obvious, next logical step* of an invention already in existence (the "prior art"). Unlike trademarks and copyrights, you aren't able to say that you have an actual "patent" in anything unless and until you file an application in the U.S. Patent and Trademark Office and receive a *Certificate of Grant of Patent*. The application must describe the invention and the inventor's claim in specific detail. Unlike a copyright, a patent covers independent development of the patented subject matter and precludes anyone from making, selling or using the invention – even if they arrive at it independently without ever seeing your invention. Unlike a trademark, a patent lasts for a limited duration – once it's expired, someone else can use the invention.

There are several types of patent applications depending on invention type and process stage. A comprehensive review of patent law is clearly beyond the scope of this book. However, for purposes of determining whether one or more of the elements of your brand is patentable, we'll focus on the three that follow:

Utility Patents cover the invention (or the improvement) of a new and useful process, machine, manufacture, or composition of matter. Owners can exclude others from making, using, or selling the invention for up to 20 years from the date of patent application filing and it requires the periodic payment of maintenance fees. Approximately 90% of patents fall under this category.

Provisional Patent Applications are filed by inventors who may not have the financial ability to file a Utility Patent but still want to protect their invention while they, e.g., obtain capital. Provisional patents must be converted to a regular Utility Patent within one year from the date that they are filed.

Design Patents are issued for a new, original, and ornamental design that is embodied in (or applied to) a product. Owners can exclude others from making, using, or selling the design for up to 15 years. Design patents do not require the payment of maintenance fees. Some elements of apparel are capable of Design Patent protection – please refer to *Chapter 5* for a discussion of same.

(C) Copyright

<u>Basics</u>. Copyright law protects originally created works that are embodied in a tangible medium of expression. Covered subject matter includes music, dramatic works, literature, visual arts, computer code, architectural plans. It is important to note that an abstract idea that is not reduced to tangible form is not covered by copyright. Moreover, in order to prove infringement, the infringing work has to be substantially similar and you have to prove that the alleged infringer had access to the original. Copyright law equips the owner with exclusive rights to reproduce his work, to prepare derivatives based on the original, to distribute copies and to publicly perform and display the work for a term of 70 years plus the life of the author.

The overall and constituent elements of your website (e.g., text/narratives, music, sound effects, film clips, photographs) and the original software code that you create or commission for purposes of operating your business are the subject of copyright law.

Copyright law also includes so-called "moral rights" which include rights of attribution (the right to be named as the author of a work) and integrity (the right to prevent others from "messing with" your work). However, unless you're the creator of a visual work of art (e.g., sculpture, paintings), it is extremely difficult to enforce these rights in the United States. (Other countries recognize them and take them seriously.) The rationale for not expanding them to all works in the U.S. is that we have other disciplines (e.g., libel, slander, misappropriation) that can be used to enforce similar rights.

Advertising & Copyright. Please have your attorney review any and all documents that are used to engage marketing and advertising agencies and anyone else who participates in the creation of your marketing campaign and website. Your contract with a photographer, agency, film producer, website designer, jingle producer etc. should specifically state that the ALL of creative works that are made in connection with your brand, marketing materials and the copyrights therein (1) are *"Works Made For Hire,"* (2) your property and (3) assigned to you. If it doesn't mention that exact phrase (and more – e.g., see *Appendix 4A*), the people who created the photograph, jingle, website look and feel, etc. are the legal owners of those works. Please be aware that this includes works created by *third party* freelancers who are engaged indirectly by your advertising or marketing agency. (So an agency needs to promise or "represent and warrant" that they have obtained all necessary rights from any freelancers.)

Problems in this area typically arise when you use *Agency A* for a campaign initially and decide (for whatever reason) to have *Agency B* complete or revise it. If you don't obtain ownership of the materials used (e.g., the code, masters, negatives, files, etc.), *Agency A* doesn't have to give them to you or *Agency B* and you won't be able to pick up where you left off. An example of a "Work for Hire" form is shown in *Appendix* 4A but again, this is not a DIY manual – the lawyer you retain to provide guidance regarding your brand and marketing efforts should be able to provide you with a form that is specifically tailored to your needs.

Architecture & Copyright. If you are engaging an architect to create a visually unique retail space, again, please have your attorney review your contract and engagement documents carefully. Architectural designs and plans are the subject of copyright law and, like the elements of an advertising campaign described above, if they are not created for, and/or assigned to, you, they are not yours to use, e.g., in the context of the expansion of your business via franchise locations and otherwise.

Music & Copyright Generally. Using sound effects on the reservations page of your website opens? A sound track as the background music for a commercial? Ambient music that provides a relaxing atmosphere for spa clients? All of these scenarios require licenses or permissions from the owners of the copyrights in the *sound recording* (what you hear when you hear the *Beatles* perform) and the underlying musical *composition* (the melodies and lyrics that *John Lennon* and *Paul McCartney* wrote and captured on sheet music). You may be able to purchase "canned" or "stock" music that is available for this purpose. If you can't find anything that is already "cleared" and suitable for your needs, you and your lawyer will have to make sure that all necessary music rights are sought and secured.

Sound Recordings. If you use a CD, downloadable file,

video recording – anything wherein a performance has been recorded or filed for playback and/or if you synchronize playback with a video that you've produced, you will have to obtain the appropriate rights from the record company to which the singer/performers are signed.

Music Composition. Whoever wrote the music that was performed on the CD/file, etc. has rights as *composer* and the right to administer and collect monies on the composer's behalf may have been sold (in part) to a *music publishing company*. You have to obtain separate permission to use the composition.

Performances. Anytime that music is played or performed publicly, "Performance Rights" are also implicated. If your business is a commercial establishment that is open to the public, it is in your best interest to obtain what's known as a "Blanket License" from the societies (ASAP, BMI, SESAC) that grant these rights on behalf of composers as well as *SoundExchange* who controls these rights on behalf of record companies– each license covers the songs in that society's repertoire for a limited number of uses during a limited period of time.

Apparel & Copyright. Copyright is not generally viewed as a means of protecting clothing and other apparel; please see the other sources of protection in *Chapter 5.*

(D) Publicity Rights

Publicity rights allow people to control their personal

identifying features – i.e., their names, likenesses and images. Unlike copyright law, and (federal) trademark law, these rights are governed by each of the 50 states. Accordingly, your ability to exploit the publicity rights of others and capitalize on the use of your own are largely dictated by the language of the contract that you enter with them.

Publicity rights are typically implicated in two common scenarios: (1) when photographs that feature other persons are used on your website and advertising materials and (2) when someone's voice is used in a radio, television or online commercial. It is easy to simply ask for permission – an example of a Consent Form is attached as *Appendix 4B*. Discuss it with your lawyer and ask that he/she create a form that is tailored for your project's needs.

Example: *You've decided to spend your first quarter profits on a magnificent ad campaign so you hire a photographer to come in and take pictures of your perfumery on a busy Saturday when the store is packed. Whose permission do you need? Answer – it depends. (a) Did your contract with the photographer state that the picture is a work for hire and that you own the copyright? (b) How old are the subjects – if any of them are minors, in addition to (c) the subject's consent, you may also have to get (d) their parent/guardian's permission as well.*

(E) Trade Secrets

Business information that is valuable because it is not

publicly available is protected under the rubric of trade secrets law. Proposals and planning materials associated with an upcoming marketing campaign or co-operative arrangement with another business (e.g., a reward that is redeemable at a complementary business) would be examples of materials that contain trade secrets in addition to other forms of intellectual property. Like publicity rights, trade secrets are generally defined and protected under state law – so they vary from state to state. Individuals and businesses will often use trade secret law to protect information that they don't want to disclose publicly via the patent application process. The most famous trade secret is probably the *Coca-Cola* formula.

A basic *Non-Disclosure Agreement ("NDA")* and Confidentiality form (an example of which is attached as *Appendix 4C*), is a starting point for guarding against disclosure by, e.g., employees and suppliers. Other suggestions include being diligent about labeling confidential information as "proprietary" and limiting disclosures to suppliers and non-involved employees. Again, this area is governed by the law of the state in which you conduct business.

Chapter 4 Take-Away Notes:

1. ***What's the difference between a Utility Patent and a Design Patent?***

2. ***How long is a Provisional Patent Application valid?***

3. ***What are the essential elements of a contract with someone who is providing creative services for, e.g. your website, your advertising campaign?***

4. ***What are the various types of copyright permissions associated with the use of music in advertising?***

5. ***Why would someone seek trade secret protection instead of a patent?***

CHAPTER 5

Protecting Fashion Brands

(A) GENERAL OVERVIEW

Imitation is the sincerest form of flattery. Sounds nice but if you're in the midst of launching a fashion brand, you would like to know that there is some way that you can protect your designs and maintain the exclusive right to call them your own. Bad news first: the functional features of apparel are not generally protectable. Now for the good news: the non-functional features of apparel (the ones that give it a certain *je ne sais quoi*) can sometimes be protected via: (1) trademark -trade dress, (2) copyright and (3) design patent.

(B) TRADE DRESS IN FASHION

Basics. As we saw in *Chapter 3,* almost anything can function as a trademark -- word, a phrase, a sound. Apparel designers should also know that various shapes, colors, patterns can also function as a three-dimensional trademark of sorts, commonly known as *trade dress.* Examples of trade dress at the center of rent court cases include the red color of a shoe-sole (*Christian Louboutin*) in *Figure 5.1* and the shape of a pocketbook (*Hermes Birkin*) in *Figure 5.2.* Identifying the features that you'd like to claim as brand signifiers is simple enough. The main thing to keep in mind is that, while you should start creating and establishing the trade dress elements of your brand on Day One, it can take years to obtain registration.

FIGURE 5.1 Exhibit - *Hermès Intn'l. v. Emperia, Inc. et al.*, 14-cv-03522 (C.D. Cal. 2014)

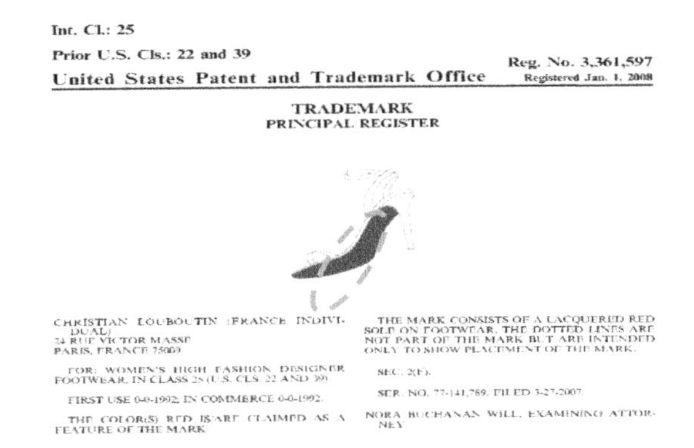

Int. Cl.: 25

Prior U.S. Cls.: 22 and 39

Reg. No. 3,361,597
Registered Jan. 1, 2008

United States Patent and Trademark Office

TRADEMARK
PRINCIPAL REGISTER

CHRISTIAN LOUBOUTIN (FRANCE INDIVIDUAL)
24 RUE VICTOR MASSE
PARIS, FRANCE 75009

FOR: WOMEN'S HIGH FASHION DESIGNER FOOTWEAR, IN CLASS 25 (U.S. CLS. 22 AND 39).

FIRST USE 0-0-1992; IN COMMERCE 0-0-1992.

THE COLOR(S) RED IS/ARE CLAIMED AS A FEATURE OF THE MARK.

THE MARK CONSISTS OF A LACQUERED RED SOLE ON FOOTWEAR. THE DOTTED LINES ARE NOT PART OF THE MARK BUT ARE INTENDED ONLY TO SHOW PLACEMENT OF THE MARK.

SEC. 2(F).

SER. NO. 77-141,789, FILED 3-27-2007.

NORA BUCHANAN WILL, EXAMINING ATTORNEY

FIGURE 5.2 Exhibit - *Christian Louboutin S.A. v. YSL Am. Inc.*, 696 F.3d 206 (2nd Cir. 2012)

Functionality. The first part of the trade dress test is met when you're able to show the USPTO that each feature you want to claim as your own is "non-functional" – i.e., that it serves no useful or necessary purpose. In the examples above, the shoe, jeans, fabric and pocket book will all function perfectly as garments if, e.g., the sole of the *Loubou* were green, the stitching on the *True Religion* jeans was in the shape of a "T," the *Burberry* fabric had circular geometric designs instead of plaid and the *Hermes* bag was heart-shaped. The use of the color red, the U-design, the plaid fabric and the shape of a *Hermes* bag are all arbitrary and random (recall *Chapter 3* and the *Spectrum of Protectability*).

Secondary Meaning. In order to claim exclusive rights to use an element of a design as trade dress, you have to be able to show that consumers associate it with your brand. How can you demonstrate this association? Key indicators of secondary meaning include: (1) significant amounts spent on advertising, (2) consumer survey results, (3) media coverage, and (4) sales – none of which are available on the day that your brand is launched.

(C) Copyright in Fashion

Copyright law protects prints, patterns, and color arrangements that are used on apparel and accessories but, in general it does not protect fashion *designs*. There is an exception for designs that incorporate "pictorial, graphic, or sculptural features that can be identified **separately** from, and (which) are capable of existing independently of, the utilitarian aspects of the article."[7]

In English, that means: if the element you want to protect can be separated from the garment physically (e.g., a fanciful belt buckle) or "conceptually," it may be copyrightable. The belt buckles in *Figure 5.1* are examples of fashion design *elements* that received copyright protection.

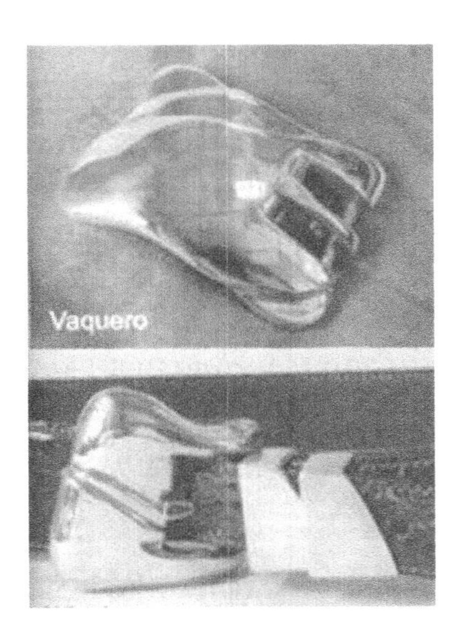

FIGURE 5.1 Exhibit *Kieselstein-Cord v. Accessories By Pearl, Inc.*, 632 F.2D 989 (2ND Cir. 1980)

(D) Design Patents in Fashion

Design patents are similar to trade dress in that, in order to obtain protection, the claimed feature cannot be functional. Unlike trade dress, a design patent will not last indefinitely[8]– they have a maximum duration **15 years**. Why then, you wonder, would someone want a design patent? For one thing, if you're a new designer and unable to establish *Secondary Meaning* as described above, a design patent may be your only option. For another, because a design patent infringement action focuses on similarity of the features to the claimed patent (as opposed to the more difficult "likelihood of confusion" standard required in trade dress cases), they are often easier to enforce. Note that like all patents, the subject of a design patent must also be new or "novel" – meaning that they can't already be in existence as part of the *"Prior Art."*

Designers like *Celine, Alexander Wang* and *Yves Saint Laurent* have protected their work via design patent. Yoga pants were the subject of a design patent case involving *Lululemon* and *Calvin Klein, Inc.* (see *Figure 5.3* below*)* and the *Apple's* now-ubiquitous large touch screen and icon layout were the subject of it's patent infringement case against *Samsung* (see *Figure 5.4.*)

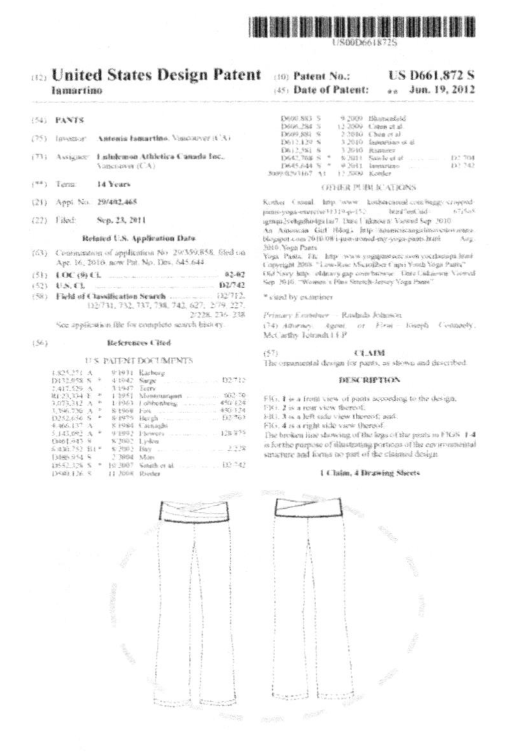

US00D661872S

(12) **United States Design Patent**
Iamartino

(10) **Patent No.:** **US D661,872 S**
(45) **Date of Patent:** ** **Jun. 19, 2012**

(54) **PANTS**

(75) Inventor: **Antonia Iamartino**, Vancouver (CA)

(73) Assignee: **Lululemon Athletica Canada Inc.**, Vancouver (CA)

(**) Term: **14 Years**

(21) Appl. No.: **29/402,465**

(22) Filed: **Sep. 23, 2011**

Related U.S. Application Data

(63) Continuation of application No. 29/359,858, filed on Apr. 16, 2010, now Pat. No. Des. 645,644.

(51) **LOC (9) Cl.** **02-02**
(52) **U.S. Cl.** **D2/742**
(58) **Field of Classification Search** D2/712, D2/731, 732, 737, 738, 742, 627; 2/79, 227, 2/228, 236-238

See application file for complete search history.

(56) **References Cited**

U.S. PATENT DOCUMENTS

OTHER PUBLICATIONS

* cited by examiner

Primary Examiner — Rashida Johnson
(74) *Attorney, Agent, or Firm* — Joseph Connolly; McCarthy Tetrault LLP

(57) **CLAIM**

The ornamental design for pants, as shown and described.

DESCRIPTION

FIG. **1** is a front view of pants according to the design.
FIG. **2** is a rear view thereof.
FIG. **3** is a left side view thereof; and
FIG. **4** is a right side view thereof.
The broken line showing of the legs of the pants in FIGS. **1-4** is for the purpose of illustrating portions of the environmental structure and forms no part of the claimed design.

1 Claim, 4 Drawing Sheets

FIGURE 5.3 Exhibit - *Lululemon Athletica CA Inc. v. Calvin Klein Inc., 1:12-cv-01034*, (D. Del.2016)

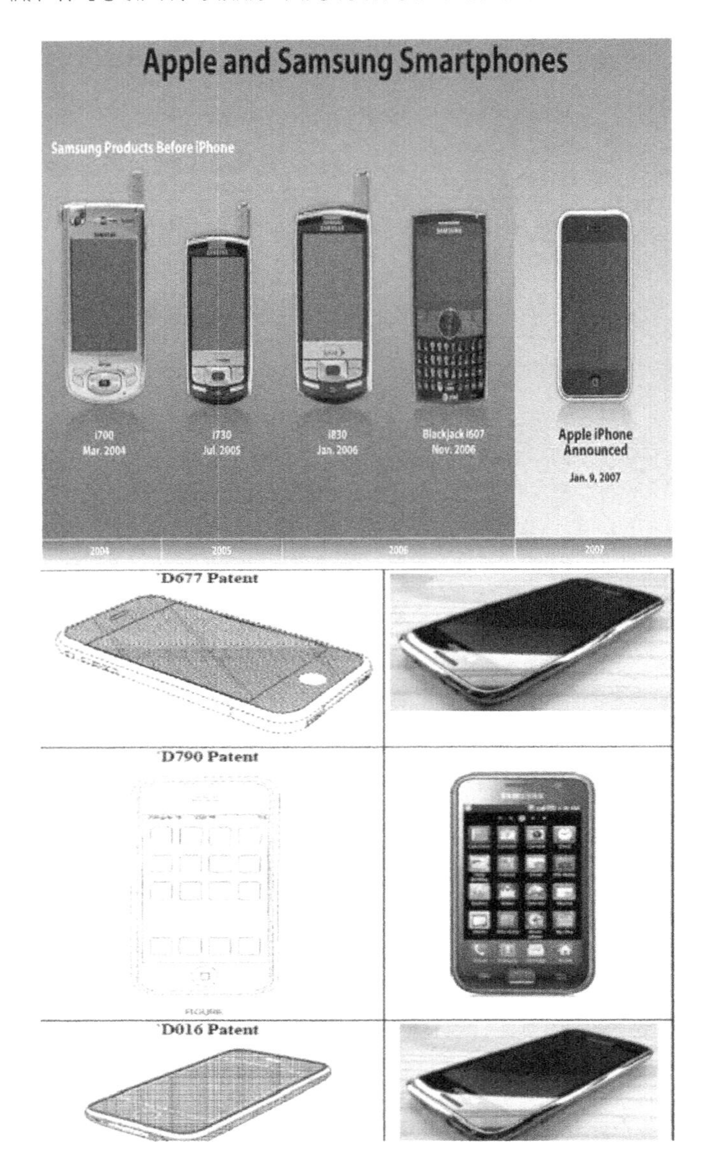

FIGURE 5.4 Exhibit – *Apple, Inc. v. Samsung Elecs., Inc.*, 678 F.3d 1314 (Fed. Cir. 2012), rev'd in part 580 U.S. __ (2016)

	Chapter 5 Take-Away Notes:
1.	***How does a fashion designer protect his/her designs?***
2.	***What is the key to obtaining Trade Dress protection?***
3.	***Does Copyright protect any element of fashion?***
4.	***How does a Design Patent differ from Trade Dress?***
5.	***List the "non-functional" features of your designs:***

---

[7] 17 U.S.C. Section 101

[8] Caveat: Once granted, trade dress registrations, like any other federal trademark registration, require routine maintenance and renewal and trade dress marks, like any other mark, must be used properly. See *Chapter 10*.

CHAPTER 6

PROTECTING ENTERTAINMENT BRANDS

(A) TITLE ENTITLEMENTS.

You've copyrighted your song, sound recording, film, book, webisode; but you want to make sure that no one else is able to use your title. Why? Because you want to deter others from trading on your hard work and usurping, e.g., the licensing, endorsement and strategic alliance opportunities that we'll discuss in upcoming chapters, that's why! Your well-intentioned friend tells you, "*not to worry, you've already got the song copyrights; all you have to do now is register the title as a trademark*!" The little bird that whispers "*a little knowledge is a dangerous thing*" should be chirping ... LOUDLY!

No Copyright Protection in Names/Titles. Titles, names, slogans and the like are not protected by copyright law. In order to garner copyright protection, a work has to contain a minimum amount of "authorship" and "original expression." You may think that your stage/band name or the title of your book/song/film is rather clever but copyright law sees them as little more than "basic facts" - the way that you identify a person or a project, nothing more. Accordingly, they don't meet Copyright's basic, statutory requirements.

Trademark Only Protects Names/Titles for a Series of Works. The Trademark Office will not protect a title of a **single** sound recording, musical composition, book, motion picture, etc. (This rule does not apply to original pieces of tangible art such as sculptures, paintings, jewelry.) You may be able to register the title as a trademark in connection with merchandise (e.g., clothing, toys) but you cannot get a trademark registration that entitles you to be the *only* person able to use, e.g. a particular album, book or film title ... unless and until you are able to show that you have used that title in connection with a **series** of works (i.e., more than one). The rationale for this restriction is that everyone, even your competitors, has to be able to describe your specific song, film, etc. When you create a series (e.g., multiple volumes, sequels/prequels, episodes), the title (e.g., "*The Fast & the Furious*") becomes a way to identify, not just *that* specific film, but also *you* as the producer, creator ... the source of the project. It doesn't matter if it's "*Los Banoleros,*" "*2 Fast 2 Furious,*" "*Turbo Charge*" – you associate each of those films as originating from the same folks who produced "*The Fast and the Furious.*" As explained in *Chapter 3,* it is that "connection" and recognition of source that a trademark is designed to protect.

This all begs the question: how *can* you protect a title after you've released it to the public but before the second version/episode/edition is released? File a trademark application based on your *intention* to use the mark in the future (i.e., an "ITU" or "intent-to-use" application discussed in *Chapter 3*.)

(B) Music/Band Issues.

The Beach Boys, En Vogue, Boston, Lynyrd Skynyrd, The Temptations, The Doors, The Platters, Sister Sledge ... the list of bands and groups who have fought over the right to continue using a well-known name after a member has left is endless. Members of any type of musical ensemble (band, group, production/writing team) must (must!) enter an agreement wherein the members hash out responsibilities, obligations and ownership of assets – now and in the future. The law can go either way; the ex members of *Boston* were able to proffer a successful fair use defense and continue using the name. The non-founding members of *En Vogue* weren't as fortunate. As a member of, and an investor in, a creative group, is this a determination that you really want to leave to the courts or an arbitration panel?

When seeking to protect a brand in the music business, it is also important to note that the same restrictions that apply to the title of a single sound recording also apply to the *name* that you perform under – you must be able to show that your discography contains more than one commercially released sound recording in order to qualify for the "series" protection described above. Again, if you're a new artist (band or individual), the way to stake claim to your name in connection with the sale of records is to file an ITU application before the second (or any) recording is released.

What if you're a solo artist using your own name or pseudonym ("p.k.a.")? You will have to file what's known as *Consent of a Living Individual* with the Trademark Office attesting to the fact that your actual/stage name refers to you and that you consent to its use and registration as a trademark. (Even if the name doesn't represent anyone who has ever lived, if it even *sounds like* it could be someone's name, the Trademark Office will require you to say "no, the name doesn't refer to anyone who has ever lived.") An example of such a form is attached as *Appendix 6A.*

Also, if your name is "John Smith," you may have to wait to get a registration for your mark in standard form (i.e., without a logo design) because common names generally require evidence of secondary meaning, described in *Chapter 3*.

(C) Motion Picture Title Protection Sources

Protect it abroad. Although the U.S. is decidedly in the "no-single-title-protection" camp, that is not a view that is shared universally. Several English speaking countries that a members of treaties with the U.S. will permit registration of a the title of a single work as a trademark.

Use a trade industry registry. Although it's certainly not a substitute for a U.S. trademark registration, registration with the Motion Picture Association of America (the "MPAA") Title Registration Bureau ("TRB") falls under the heading "it's better-than-nothing." The primary shortcoming with the TRB is that you have to become a subscribing member in order to use it as a way to protect your title and then, its reach is limited to ... other subscribers. Nevertheless, it has (baby) teeth. Ever wonder why the 2013 bio-drama that starred Oprah Winfrey was entitled "*Lee Daniels'* The Butler" (and not just "The Butler")? It's because of a 1916 Warner Brother's film that had been registered with the TRB.

(D) 360 Deals[9] and Brand Control

Three-sixty deals, as the name implies, refer to agreements (typically recording contracts) wherein the record label obtains rights that extend beyond those that are necessary to create and promote records (i.e., beyond the reproduction, distribution and derivative works copyright entitlements that form the basis for every recording contract). When an artist/band signs a 360 deal, they are typically giving the label the right to own/participate in other income generating sources – e.g., merchandise (discussed in *Chapter 12*), touring/sponsorship (discussed in *Chapter 14*), publishing (discussed in *Chapters 4* and 6), etc. There's nothing new about these deals; indeed, it was commonly understood in the music industry that if you wanted a record deal with a label that I engaged with on a regular basis in the 1990's, you were *going* to enter a publishing deal with that label's affiliated publishing company. What *is* new is that these deals have now dominated the music industry and ... they have gained popularity in other areas of entertainment and creative business in general.

Are they good? Are they bad? I'm certainly not going to be the one to tell you to pass on a 360 offer if you need the advance in order to keep your lights on. But the fact that so many music artists are successfully choosing to go the independent route speaks volumes about technological changes in the marketplace and one's ability to monetize intellectual property while retaining control of it at the same time.

One thing I'm adamant about is obtaining trademark registrations in your own name – particularly for the name of your band and the name that you use e.g., when performing, writing, posting, streaming, etc. If you can afford the costs associated with clearing and registering these trademark assets, do so; I can't see any good reason (other than expense) to have another person or entity register your name. When pressed, companies will accept a grant of rights (or a "license") to *use* the name as opposed to insisting upon an outright conveyance of ownership. Even if they are footing the bill for the clearance and registration, compensate them using another method (e.g., royalty/participation points, first right of refusal for ancillary deals, etc.) … but don't just relinquish *ownership* of your name.

	Chapter 6 Take-Away Notes:
1.	***True or False:*** *Copyright Law is the best way to protect a title of a book, song or film?*
2.	***True or False:*** *the only way to use trademark law to protect your name as an artist or the name of a band is to register the title of each song that you record separately, as they are released?*
3.	***True or False:*** *"ITU" is an abbreviation for "Intermittent Trademark Unit"?*
4.	***True or False:*** *the only way to sell records is by entering a "360 Deal" with a major label?*
5	***True or False:*** *the only way to protect the name of a film is by registering it with the Director's Guild?*

[9] An in-depth review of the subject is Kendall A. Minter, Esq.'s *UNDERSTANDING AND NEGOTIATING 360 ANCILLARY RIGHTS DEALS: AN ARTIST'S GUIDE TO NEGOTIATING 360 RECORD DEALS (NAM CHI 2015).*

CHAPTER 7

Online Sales & Brand Usage

(A) SELLING PRODUCTS ("TANGIBLE GOODS") ONLINE.

In order to register a trademark in the USPTO, you must first meet the statutory "use" requirement described above in *Chapter 3*; you have to show via evidence that you are not just casually mentioning your mark, but that you are actually "using it **as a trademark**." This evidence (or "specimen") requirement stumps many trademark owners who sell or intend to sell products on the Internet via their websites. (The bar for using a webpage to support a claim for a service mark in connection with, e.g., film editing, beauty care, or education services is much lower and far less troublesome.)

To recap key concepts introduced in *Chapter 3*, acceptable specimens of use for products are usually labels, tags or packaging for the products. An acceptable specimen can also be a portal that is used for simultaneously displaying (or describing) the products with the trademark and offering them for sale - that is how websites are used to support a trademark application.

The USPTO examines website pages with a monocle and a microscope. An exaggeration of course but, when submitting a webpage as evidence of use in support of a trademark application, the examination is not cursory. The website page must show each of the following: (1) a picture (or detailed description) of the product(s) that are covered in the application, (2) prominent use of the mark that indicates a close association with the products, and (3) a means for ordering the products. (See *Appendix 7-A*.) Sounds simple?

The first requirement, a _picture_ or detailed description of the products claimed in the application is self-explanatory. It is the second requirement, "association" between the mark and the products that causes delays and results in … (cough) some very colorful discussions with web-designers. To create the necessary association, the overall impression of the submitted webpage must create a consumer nexus (an immediate connection) between your mark and your products. There are two factors that are used in making this determination: (1) the prominence of the trademark and (2) the placement of the trademark.

"_Prominence_" is a relative term based on what surrounds the mark. A "prominent" mark is usually shown in a larger or more stylistic font than other text on the page. Even though it pertains to placement, a prominent mark is usually displayed at the start of a line (as opposed to the middle or the end).

"_Placement_" is straightforward: the mark should be directly adjacent to, or included in, the picture (or description) of the products that are covered by the application. It is also well-known that Examiners in the PTO will make certain assumptions based on the graphic location of the mark on the webpage – inclusion in a URL domain name is just a way to tell the consumer where they've arrived on the Internet, nothing more. Similarly, use of the mark only at the top of the page (and not close to the products) is often viewed as service mark usage – i.e., it would be sufficient for "online retail clothing store services" in class 35; it would not pass muster if you wanted to claim the actual "hats and coats" in class 25. Finally, in terms of placement, the use of multiple trademarks on the same webpage is said to distract the consumer and impede the connection between the trademark and the products.

The final requirement, providing a means for "*ordering*" the product, is straightforward but, because clients are often on a quest to imbue artistic elements in their websites, it's been known to cause a bit of web-designer dismay as well. A good rule to follow is the two-second rule: after opening the page, if it takes longer than two seconds to click (or dial) and order the product, the page is relegated to mere advertisement status – it will not be considered a way to purchase the products and it probably won't meet the USPTO's use requirements.

(B) Offering & Promoting Services Online

Compared to the use requirements for products, the use requirements for services that are sold or promoted online are a walk in the park. *Figure 7.1* is a screenshot from a specimen of use submitted in support of the application to register MARKS FOR MUSIC MOVIES AND MORE as a service mark for brand consultation and legal services.

FIGURE 7.1 WWW.MARKSFORMUSICMOVIESANDMORE.COM

The primary requirement is that the specimen of use must (a) display the mark (shown in the large dotted circle) prominently and (b) describe (or at least reference) the services (as shown in the smaller dotted circle). USPTO guideline examples for submitting specimens in support of brands for entertainment and technology services are provided in *Appendix 7B.*

Helpful Tip: *Discuss these requirements with your graphic and website designers during your early meetings. (You don't want to give them a necessary but labor-intensive revision request at the last minute.) Please (please) make sure that your website is live and not "under construction" or "to be announced" when it is submitted to the Trademark Office as evidence of the current use of your trademark.*

Chapter 7 Take-Away Notes:

1. ***What are the two factors that are used to determine whether there's a sufficient association between the trademark on a website and the products claimed in a trademark application?***

2. **True or False:** *it's easier to use a website as evidence of use for services than for products.*

3. **True or False:** *registering your website URL will protect your company name as well.*

4. **True or False:** *using your company name in your URL will satisfy the Trademark Office's use requirements.*

5. **True or False:** *using your company name in social media will satisfy the Trademark Office's use Requirements.*

CHAPTER 8

RETAIL SPACES & PROTECTING TRADE DECOR

Overview. In *Chapter 3,* we discussed trademark basics and noted that it is possible to have trademark protection in almost anything – even a sound. In *Chapter 7,* we discussed the ever-changing world of online retail and ways that an online proprietor can use his/her website to support trademark registrations for the products he/she sells. Now, we're making a wide left turn – back to the future of retail: brick and mortar stores that cater to the online shopper's needs. Brands like *Apple* and *Walmart* are recognizing the pivot from "showrooming" to "webrooming" – where consumers browse online before heading in-store to touch and see products before actual purchases are made.

It's no coincidence that the "flowery -musk" scent you experience as you enter, linger, inquire and upgrade in the *Verizon* store reminds you of your last vacation; that scent is protected by U.S. Trademark Registration No. 4,618,936. Similarly, if you feel a little more centered and less harried as you browse the latest offerings in the *Apple* store, Zen-props are owed to the oblong (as opposed to rectangular) minimalist tables and flush mounted (as opposed to angular) mounted video screens that comprise U.S. Trademark Registration No. 4,227,914. Does your appetite grow to Ralph Kramden or Archie Bunker upon entering *Chipotle*? Who can blame you when you're surrounded by the galvanized steel, rivets and industrial lamps that comprise U.S. Trademark Registration No. 4,075,479.

Before submitting an application for weathered driftwood tables and the living walls you envision for your farm-to-table tapas bar, note that obtaining trade dress protection requires two things: time and success. You can't be in a rush and you must establish a following that associates those special features with your brand.

Trade dress in the retail environment (i.e., restaurants, stores, banks, etc.) was recognized by the Supreme Court in the context of two elaborately decorated Mexican restaurants, *Two Pessos* and *Taco Cabana* pictured in *Figure 8.1*.

FIGURE 8.1 Exhibit *Two Pesos v. Taco Cabana*, 505 U.S. 763 (1992)

Since then, the standards of protection and the hurdles that must be climbed in order to obtain trade dress protection in general have been fleshed-out in cases involving consumer products giants *Walmart, Volkswagen* and others. It's a complicated (and intriguing) area of intellectual property but the hurdles are summarized as (1) *functionality* and (2) *secondary meaning*.

Functionality. Everyone - you, me, your competitors - has to be able to use design features that are functional; i.e., those are the features that are essential or "functional" in the provision of goods and services. For example, in a case involving wine merchant *Best Cellars,* a court ruled that certain elements of their décor (e.g., the placement of information cards in front of wine bottles and horizontal stacking racks) were purely functional and utilitarian. (Fortunately for Best Cellars, there were other elements of their décor that were deemed to be deserving of protection.)

Secondary Meaning. Did you survive functionality review? You are in the home-stretch – halfway there depending on your idea of a long time. You will now have to demonstrate to the PTO's satisfaction that consumers recognize your décor as yours, and yours alone – in your line of business. You will have to present proof of advertising expenditures as well as evidence of media/press coverage of the unique decor features (e.g., a recording of Channel 76's feature story on the living wall in your farm-to-table restaurant or the reclaimed wood floors in your boutique). It's also more likely than not that you'll be asked to complete and present the results of an expensive consumer survey; i.e., you will have to ask a representative sampling of consumers in your relevant market, e.g., "*what/who do you think of when you walk in a restaurant and see antique wallpaper and World War II memorabilia*" and pray that they associate those things with your brand.

What if you aren't able to establish Secondary Meaning? You have two choices: remain patient or accept relegation to the *Supplemental Register* (discussed in *Chapter* 3.) For example, *Stuart Weitzman* has a supplemental registration for "a retail store interior with a color white ribbon pattern ... making up the design of table, counters and chairs."

Helpful Tip: *Be practical. The trade dress design process is long and tedious; it is not for the indecisive or the faint of pocket or heart. If your business is new and you have a unique design that you want to protect, you might want to first consider seeking protection of, e.g., the overall look and feel of your website and certain articles that you sell.*

Chapter 8 Take-Away Notes:

1. ***List three unique features of your current retail decor (or a future location if your current focus is a line of products sold online or by others in their retail locations):***

2. ***Look at your answer(s) to #1 above. Identify and describe the non-functional elements of your decor:***

3. ***What can you use (in the way of advertising, collected data/metrics, etc.) to establish consumer association (i.e., Secondary Meaning) with your brand?***

CHAPTER 9

INTERNATIONAL BRANDS

Where will your brand be used? Because of the Internet, market borders simply aren't what they used to be. The reality is that some countries, e.g., China and other so-called "first to file" countries have laws that favor the first person to file an application – regardless of whether or not they have ever actually used it. As a result, U.S. owners of famous brands (e.g., *Apple, Michael Jordan, Ferrari*) can face an uphill battle if an application is already on file for THEIR marks in one of these countries. Accordingly, and especially when dealing with apparel and related accessories, it's a good idea to file an application in China where counterfeiting is legion. Other good choices are countries where the same language is spoken – e.g., if you're a U.S. trademark owner, you are well advised to extend protection to the United Kingdom, South Africa, Canada and other English speaking countries – especially if your mark is comprised entirely of English words.

There are basically two ways to extend protection to countries beyond the United States – your attorney can file a collaborative application via the World Intellectual Property Organization's ("WIPO's") Madrid International Trademark System or you can file "locally" – i.e., via a trademark agent who is actually located in China, South Africa, Mexico, etc. The treaty vs. local filing decision usually hinges on costs and the complexity of the mark.

A word about "Priority Rights" – you have six months from the date that your U.S. application is filed to extend protection to another member country and still be able to claim the original U.S. filing date. If you have concerns about parties located in other countries who are using your mark without authorization, this is an important deadline that you don't want to miss.

	Chapter 9 Take-Away Notes:
1	***List the languages that your core customers speak:***
2.	***List the countries where these languages are spoken:***
3.	***If you are selling apparel or electronics, which country (ies) should you absolutely consider filing in - in addition to the U.S.?***

PART III

PROPER USE

CHAPTER 10

Displaying & Using Your Brand

<u>*Use **YOUR** Mark*</u>. The actual mark. The one that is the subject of your trademark application/registration. Don't add in words like "International," "Management," "& Friends," etc. if you didn't include them in your application. If you really want to change the mark by, e.g., adding an additional word or changing the color of a logo – file a new application and register the new mark.

Having to use your mark doesn't seem like a big deal? Well, if you go back to *Chapter 3*, you'll recall that "use" is a critical requirement for trademark registration in the United States. Please note that use will continue to be an essential part of trademark ownership and maintenance – throughout the life of your brand. In the first place, when you file the maintenance and renewal documents discussed in *Chapter 17*, you'll have to include evidence of continued use of your mark – exactly as you've registered it. Moreover, you can be challenged by a third party (e.g., in a cancellation proceeding covered in *Chapter 18*) for abandonment or inexcusable non-use of your mark if you cease to use it consistently.

<u>*Be Special, Never Generic*</u>. We discussed the bane of trademark existence otherwise known as "genericness" in *Chapter 3*. Failing to guard against generic use can result in the loss of your trademark rights – e.g., "Elevator" was once a trademark and now it is the word that Americans use to refer to all "lifts." The general rule to remember is that your trademark should always be used as an adjective, never as a noun (for products) and never as a verb (for services). The table below sets forth the comparison; it is also helpful to remember that "A" is

for "Always" and "Adjective" and "**N**e**V**er" contains an "N" for "Noun" and a "V" for "Verb.

Table 10-1 – Proper Use

Right:	**Wrong:**
Pass the **KLEENEX** tissues please.	Pass the **KLEENEX** please.
Put a **BAND-AID** adhesive strip on it.	Put a **BAND-AID** on it.
Send it via a **FED EX** shipping method for delivery tomorrow.	**FED EX** it for delivery tomorrow.
You can make 10 **XEROX** copies of a document in 1 second.	You can **XEROX** 10 copies of a document in 1 second.

Use Symbols Properly. In *Chapter 3*, we touched upon the various symbols that are used to indicate whether a word or symbol is registered and/or pending registration as a trademark. The following table sets forth each of the symbols that you may have reason to use in the course of building your business, advertising, promotions, interacting with suppliers, etc.

Table 10-2 – Use of Symbols

Symbol:	**Meaning:**
®	Registered trademark (i.e., you've received the Certificate of Registration).
TM	Unregistered trademark or application pending, user is claiming exclusive right to use it on goods/products.
SM	Unregistered service mark or application pending, user is claiming exclusive right to use it on services.
Ⓟ	Patented invention (i.e., you've received the Certificate of Grant of Patent).
Patent Pending	An application is on file in the Patent Office.
©	Copyrighted work. Symbol should be followed by date of creation, name of author (creator) and the phrase "All Rights Reserved."

The appropriate trademark symbol should be **adjacent** to and immediately following the word or symbol that comprises your trademark. Examples are provided in ***Figure 10.1*** below:

Symbol Placement Example:	Mark registered in the USPTO:	Notes:
Acme Shipping & Parcel®	Word Mark: "ACME SHIPPING & PARCEL".	Registration symbol is placed in subscript position next to last letter of the mark.
Acme® Shipping & Parcel	Word Mark: "ACME"	Registration symbol is placed in superscript position next to last letter of the mark.
 ®	Logo-Design Mark: a two-dimensional outline in black and white of a walking dog.	Registration symbol is placed in subscript position next to mark.
 ACME® ®	Word Mark: "ACME". Logo-Design Mark: a two-dimensional outline in black and white of a walking dog.	Registration symbol is placed in superscript position next to last letter of the mark. Registration symbol is placed in subscript position next to mark

Similarly, the patent symbol or the words *Patent Pending* should be in an obvious location (e.g., near the serial or model number) on inventions for which you have sought/obtained patent protection.

Display. Use font coloring, size, position or background color blocking to distinguish your trademark from the other information on your packaging, website, store displays, printed materials, etc.

Online Use. Please refer to *Chapter 7*.

	Chapter 10 Take-Away Notes:
1.	**True or False:** *one way to avoid "genericness" is to always use your mark as a noun.*
2.	***Choose a word from the list below that can be added to your mark without compromising the consistency of your use:***
	a. "International"
	b. "Productions"
	c. (Your Geographic Location – e.g., "NYC")
	d. None of the above.

Chapter 11

Remarks About Parodies

You can tell by the title of this chapter that I have mixed feelings about parodies. When they are clever, they can tug at a would-be customer's heartstrings and garner instant recognition of your product line. It's just that, even when they are good (something that you can't take for granted for the reasons outlined below), you're always in someone else's shadow. If the original mark loses traction in the pop culture race, where does that leave you?

If you're set on using a tongue-in-cheek parody reference for your brand, be forewarned, if you don't get it right, you will have wasted a lot of time, effort and money. Undaunted? Okay, here's what you need to know: First and foremost, understand that a trademark parody is basically a *defense* to trademark infringement. It's a way of responding to the target of the parody and saying *"no, I'm not infringing your mark, I'm expressing socially useful commentary."*

Examples of trademark parodies that were successfully defended when challenged by original/target brand owner *Louis Vuitton* are shown in *Figures 11.1* and *11.2* below. When viewed in a side by side comparison with *LV's* protected trade dress and insignia, it's easy to understand the parody analysis conducted by the Second and Fourth Circuit Courts of Appeal.

FIGURE 11.1Exhibits - *Louis Vuitton Malletier S.A. v. Haute Diggity Dog, LLC*, 507 F.3d 252 (4th Cir., 2007)

FIGURE 11.2. Exhibits - *Louis Vuitton Malletier, S. A. v. My Other Bag, Inc.*, No. 16-241-cv (2nd Cir. 2016)

Haute Diggity makes dog chew toys that resemble famous luxury brands, including *Chewnel No. 5, Jimmy Chew, Dog Perignonn, Sniffany & Co.* and … *Chewy Vuitton*, pictured above. The other case involved *My Other Bag Inc.'s*, bag, also pictured above, wherein the inference is that the wearer's "other bag" is a (real) *Louis Vuitton.* The Second and the Fourth Circuit courts sent *LV* packing using a parody analysis that included the following:

- ❖ Is the Parody similar enough to the original to clearly communicate that it is an imitation and yet, does it also communicate some degree of satire, ridicule, joking or amusement. (Look at the figures above – do you agree that both cases involved a degree of satire? I would have to say "yes" on both.)

- ❖ Is the original a strong, i.e., "popular" brand? Ironically, this factor actually weighs *in support* of a parody and a finding that the original has *not* been infringed. Why? The theory is that if the original is instantly recognizable, the consumer is *aware* of the parody so … he's *less* likely to confuse the defendant's parody products with the originals. I've had at least one *LV* article in wardrobe rotation (a purse, wallet, planner, key chain, heck, a hair clip since I was in high school and … I'm not a designer-loyalist or fanatic; accordingly, from a personal perspective, I would have to give the "popularity" prong of the analysis a resounding "yes" in the context of both parody cases.

- Are the products distinctive and are they sold in distinctive channels of trade? If they are, that weighs in the parody's favor because it won't be competing with the original for sales. Here's where I look at the *My Other Bag* and *Chewy* cases differently. *Louis Vuitton* has an established line of pet products – I once received an *LV* collar for my dog as a gift and I coveted the pet carrying case that was about a half-inch too short for the dog I had at the time. Accordingly, it's not unreasonable to think that, if I'd also wanted a dog chew toy, I might splurge at the LV shop on a chew toy – like the one at the heart of the *Chewy Vuitton* case. Accordingly, I've always thought that this factor weighed in *Louis Vuitton's* favor. In contrast, I don't think the same is true regarding *My Other Bag*; I don't see how/where luxury bags costing hundreds, often thousands, of dollars competes with a whimsical, glorified grocery store bag – but for the use of the *LV* designs, it has a similar appearance and the same type of construction as the ones that you purchase for $1.49 at check-out.

There's more to it than just ticking off the three boxes above – the exact context (e.g., the composition of the marketplace) in which you are considering the use of a parody mark should be evaluated by your attorney … BEFORE you start using it.

	Chapter 11 Take-Away Notes:
1.	***If you're considering a parodic mark, list the ways that your products/services are (a) similar. to and (b) different from the subject of the parody:***
2.	***What is your target audience and why/how will the significance of the parody be recognized?***
3.	***Is the relevance of the subject of the parody limited in the context of your products/services?***
4.	***In the future, is it reasonable to assume that the target would sell products/services that are similar to yours?***

PART IV

POSITIONING

CHAPTER 12

Licenses & Distribution

Once all the rights in the intellectual property comprising your brand are registered and secured, the next step is exploiting or leveraging your brand. If the brand is well known, you will either be approached by, or find it easy to get an audience with, larger companies interested in using your brand in a way that is different than your initial use (e.g., you manufacture clothing and a company approaches you about a license to manufacture jewelry under your brand). Alternatively, the conversation may be about distributing your products in regions that are beyond the area that you currently serve. At the heart of each such agreement is a basic license where you're the licensor (i.e., the owner of the brand) and the person you're granting the license to is the licensee.

(A) LICENSES

The benefit of a license arrangement for the brand owner (the "Licensor") is minimal involvement and oversight; once a deal is done and the product ships, the manufacturer (the "Licensee") takes the ball over the finish line and the Licensor is out of the picture. The downside is the other side of the same coin – unless a Licensor wields the leverage to demand approval rights and set usage standards, he loses control of the end-product, the way the brand is displayed, where it is sold, etc.

Merchandise Agreements (Licenses) generated over $250B in revenue in 2015. At its core, a "*Merchandise Deal*" is a license wherein a brand owner (e.g., a designer, producer/film studio, music artist/label, inventor, athlete, etc.) enters an agreement with a manufacturing company to produce goods that the brand owner doesn't have the capability and/or the desire to produce. In exchange for being able to use brand-related intellectual property (e.g., a trademark consisting of a person's name, a character from a film, the name of another brand in another line of business, a design or logo), the manufacturing company pays the brand owner either an upfront payment upon signing, a percentage of sales (a royalty) or a combination of both.

i. GENERAL LICENSE FORMS & TERMS

Licenses can range from a single page deal memo to a 1,000 page complex document with hundreds of exhibits, schedules and appendices. Nevertheless, the core elements of a license are the same:

Scope. This is the first element that I look at: how is the subject matter (i.e., the brand, trademark, character, etc.) defined? What does it include? What does it exclude?

Term and Exclusivity. How long with the license last and during that time, is the Licensee the only company that will have the right to use, e.g., the character?

Money. How much is the Licensee going to pay Licensor and in what measure – a royalty per item, guaranteed minimum, advance against royalties, percentage of sales (net/gross), etc.?

Options/Renewal. If this works out well (i.e., in terms of dollar figures), who will have the right to exercise an option to renew and/or will the agreement be extended automatically?

Quality and Use of Brand/Mark/Character. Can Licensor count on the licensee to produce a quality product and will the Licensor protect and use the licensed asset in a manner that is consistent with the licensor's reputation?

ii. FILM MERCHANDISE

Merchandise opportunities are generally sought and obtained in the action, animation, musical and youth oriented genres like *Star Wars* ($32B in merchandise revenue to date), *Harry Potter* ($7B), and *Frozen* ($5.3B). These tie-ins extend to every product/service line imaginable (e.g., *Harry Potter* wizard-fans can now cool off with a helping of *"ButterBeer"* ice cream, courtesy of *Yuenling*, the famous brewery turned confectioner-glacier). However, because revenue from merchandise is often used to offset film production costs and because sales of branded products like apparel, cosmetics, costumes and novelty items can simultaneously have the incidental effect of promoting the underlying film prior to its release, proponents of more serious films (and programs) aren't sleeping on merchandise as a source of income. (*Amazon.com's* various offerings connected with *50 Shades of Grey* include a signature *Vermont Teddy Bear*, a limited edition *OPI Nail Collection* set comprised of five grey and one red nail shades, signature wines gift sets, a board game, etc. (Products that *appear* to be unauthorized and lurking in the shadows of a parody defense include baby onesies that reference a mother's reading session nine months prior.)

iii. Fashion Merchandise

Tom Ford's foray into retail products sold under his own name was far simpler than it would have been because, instead of manufacturing fragrances and sunglasses himself, he wisely entered license agreements with established cosmetics and eyewear companies - *Estee Lauder* and *Marcolin*. In sports, *Major League Baseball's ("MLB")* recently announced a license arrangement with *Jessica Alba's Honest Company* wherein *Honest Company* will imprint licensed *MLB* logos on *Honest* diapers and sell them in big box stores like *Target*; the goal, according to MLB representatives is to develop baseball fan loyalty – early. From *Honest's* perspective, the team logos will appeal to parents who are serious fans of the team brands that are included in the deal – among them, the *New York Yankees* (!) and the *Boston Red Sox* (?)

An example of a licensing deal gone awry is the one that *Calvin Klein* had with *Warnaco* where the latter produced products without *Calvin Klein's* authorization and the result was that the unauthorized products competed with, and tarnished, authentic products within the *Calvin Klein* brand.

(B) DISTRIBUTION

There are almost as many ways to sell products to the public as there are stores. If distribution is on the horizon, you should note the following types of arrangements – the terms and conditions of which are often combined and modified to suit specific business needs, budgetary constraints, and logistical limitations:

White Label Products are made by a manufacturer on a non-exclusive basis and rebranded as you, the brand owner, deems necessary and appropriate.

Private Label Products are manufactured in-house or for a brand owner's exclusive use (e.g., one of *Target's* private labels for food is *Archer Farms, Costco* uses the *Kirkland* name to sell foods as well as apparel).

Showrooms are places where a brand owner displays its products for viewing and purchase by wholesale buyers with whom the showroom has relationships.

Consignment Agreements where a store owner agrees to display and sell products in exchange for a percentage of sales when the products are sold; it is not confined to use in second hand stores – they are a way to minimize risks for both the store owner and the brand owner.

Wholesale Price is the reduced price offered to distributors and/or store owners and it's based on volume discounts.

Manufacturing Agreements, as the name implies, are for the production of products.

Distribution Agreements are between the brand owner and the so-called middle men who have relationships with retailers and brand owners to introduce these parties and negotiate on behalf of the brand owner.

	Chapter 12 Take-Away Notes:
1.	***True or False***: *Brand owners choose license arrangements when they want to retain maximum control over licensed products.*
2.	***Which of the following are contractual terms that should be considered when presenting or reviewing a licensing arrangement?*** *(a) Scope and Options/Renewal* *(b) Manufacturing and Distribution* *(c) Term/Exclusivity and Amount of Fee* *(d) Quality Control and Use of Brand*

Chapter 13

Franchises

(A) General Overview

Most people associate the word "franchise" with fast food restaurants but brand owners in all lines of business can and do offer franchises – e.g., hotels (*Marriott* and *Hilton*), real estate brokerages (*Century 21, Coldwell Banker*), cosmetic/day spas (*Merle Norman*). A franchise is to service businesses what a license agreement is for tangible products; indeed, a trademark license is an integral part of a franchise relationship between the franchisor (the owner of the brand / service business e.g., a dry cleaners or restaurant) and the franchisee (the person who is paying a fee for the privilege of being able to open a business under and already established name.)

Franchise Law is another nuanced legal discipline where it's a good idea to consult a specialist.[10] If you are the franchisor, in addition to the trademark license, you are required to comply with specific disclosure requirements as well as registration in each state that requires pre-registration before a franchise can be offered for sale or opened for business. Failure to comply with all of these strict requirements can mean business failure and financial ruin if you're not careful.

Because of the importance that the trademark plays in the context of franchises (i.e., it's literally at the core of every franchise), this is a business expansion activity that you should postpone until your essential trademarks are protected in accordance with the guidelines set forth in *Chapter 3.*

(B) FRANCHISING YOUR BRAND

There are three (3) elements at the core of any franchise arrangement and if you have them, you have created a franchise (whether you intended to or not): (a) a **trademark license** running from the brand owner (the "Franchisor") to the person buying into the franchise (the "Franchisee"), (b) the payment of a **fee** to the Franchisor and (c) the Franchisee's adherence to the Franchisor's prescribed **business methodology**. Don't miss this: if a brand owner's relationship with another person or business involves these three elements, the business relationship is a *de facto* franchise. Franchise owners are required to comply – under threat of criminal and civil liability - with all applicable Federal Trade Commission ("FTC") and state rules and regulations. These rules can be extremely onerous and expensive to adhere to. They include, e.g., the preparation and specifically timed distribution of intricate disclosure documents (known as a "Franchise Disclosure Document" or "FDD") and an operations manual (commonly referred to as an "Employee Handbook").

The benefit of a franchise arrangement for the brand owner is that he will have a great deal of control over the way that the Franchisee uses the brand and operates the franchise. The downside is the other side of the same coin - the Franchisor is required to actively supervise and guide the efforts of its Franchisees.

(C) BECOMING THE FRANCHISEE OF A BRAND

If you are considering the purchase of a new or established franchise, please do your due diligence. You don't want to be in a situation where you're liable for using a brand name that isn't the Franchisor's to share. Similarly, you don't want to risk investing in a franchise that centers around a brand name that isn't exclusive to the franchise. If your budget allows, invest in a trademark search described in *Chapter 3* above. You're not going to use it to file an application for the Franchise trademark – that right generally belongs to the franchisor alone and the trademark license that you are signing will probably prohibit you from registering trademarks that are identical or similar to any of the franchise's trademarks. However, you'll want to assess the "health" of the brand's trademark portfolio *before* you commit yourself to using it.

Another challenge that Franchisees can face in the context of intellectual property in general and trademarks in particular is compliance with the usage guidelines that are a part of the franchise's trademark license. These guidelines should be committed to memory and referenced when, e.g., designing a website, ordering signage – even disposing of products and materials wherein the franchise's trademarks and logos appear. Remember also that the appearance of various elements of a physical location comprise the franchise's intellectual property and trade decor discussed in *Chapter 8* (e.g., the paint on the walls of a restaurant that is the same shade of red worn by the wait-staff). Depending on the franchise, some or all of the products and materials that are used in operating a franchise may have to be purchased internally or from a designated vendor. If décor guidelines give the Franchisee the ability to purchase materials externally – as long as they comply with the franchises specifications – then make sure that they are in compliance.

	Chapter 13 Take-Away Notes:
1.	***What are the characteristics of your business*** *that comprise your brand? (E.g., unique/private label products, centralized customer service, rigorous management standards and training, trade secrets like recipes and chemical ingredients or processes.) Hint: review your notes in Chapters 1 and 2.*
2.	**List the reasons why you believe your current store/space is successful (e.g., close to a campus, church, hospital, older/younger demographic, owner/renter neighborhood).**
3.	***Make an honest assessment of your ability to increase your responsibilities for management, vendor/supplier relationships, employee dispute resolution, training, etc. … exponentially!!***

•

---

[10] Two resources that provide a solid overview of the area are the *FRANCHISE BIBLE: HOW TO BUY A FRANCHISE OR FRANCHISE YOUR OWN BUSINESS,* Erwin J. Keup (2004) and *THE FRANCHISE MBA: MASTERING THE 4 ESSENTIAL STEPS TO OWNING A FRANCHISE,* Rick Grossman & Michael J. Katz (2013)

Chapter 14

Collaborative Efforts – Endorsers/Influencers, Sponsors & Strategic Alliance Partners

(A) General Overview

"This above all: to thine own self be true ..."
~ William Shakespeare (Hamlet Act I, Sc. 3)

If I had to identify just one thing that the most successful sponsorships, endorsements and strategic alliances always seem have – in droves, it's ruthless, unapologetic *brand awareness*. In the way that a great performer knows exactly what it is that he brings to a production as well as his limitations, the astute brand owner (or manager) is aware of his brand's value and position as well as the areas where there's an opportunity for improvement, expansion, development etc. In making an honest assessment of both your brand and your prospective endorser, sponsor or strategic alliance collaborator, there are at least five areas that must be evaluated:

- ***Demographics** and market **share** – actual, targeted and barriers.*
- *Access to **media** – traditional and social.*
- ***Fame/Notoriety** – both of which are relative in the context of contemplated products and services.*
- ***ROI** or **value** of increased market presence resulting from the collaboration.*
- ***New product or service** capabilities resulting directly from the collaboration and the allocation of ownership/control of each.*

(B) Endorsers & Influencers

Using celebrities to promote products is a time-honored, proven way to boost sales (e.g., *Michael Jordan's* long standing relationship with *Nike*). In addition to trademark rights, celebrity endorsements also implicate *Rights of Privacy* and *Rights of Publicity*. Now's a good time to note that, in the same way that all politics are local, all celebrity is "relative;" if someone has a few thousand followers on social media, they may not be a *household* brand in the full sense of the word but, depending on the composition of their followers (e.g., primarily college educated, professionals who own a home, have children, are located in major metropolitan areas, etc.), their "celebrity" may be desirable and influential for a specific product or line of business.

The compensation structure of endorsement agreements can take many forms including upfront payments like the one that *Justin Bieber* is said to have received from *OPI* for his signature *"One Less Lonely Girl"* nail polish collection. In this example, OPI departed from the typical endorsement model wherein an endorser actually uses the brand (e.g., *Oprah Winfrey* losing weight with *Weight Watchers*, *Jennifer Aniston* protect her eyes *EyeLove* drops); OPI's goal was to obtain pin-pointed exposure to the brand's target market - millions of young, female *Bieber* followers and fans. Other celebrities, like *Kim Kardashian*, are parties to *net profit sharing arrangements* wherein they receive a percentage of sales; e.g., *Kardashian* receives 45% of the net profits earned in connection with the app game formerly known as *Stardom: The A List*, now aptly titled

Kim Kardashian: Hollywood. Yet another payment model is structured more like an annual salary.

In addition to compensation, the contractual relationship between brand (product) owner and the endorser generally addresses several issues, among them:

Exclusivity & Use of Product. If a brand pays someone to wear and/or use a branded product, they expect them to … wear and/or use it! Instances where celebrities didn't "dance with the guy who brought them to the party" include *Charlize Theron* wearing a *Dior* watch in ads (and in her down time) despite the fact that she was party to contract to endorse *Raymond Weil* watches at the time; *Manny Pacquaio,* a *Samsung* spokesperson, using his *IPhone* to *Tweet*; and the absolute best of the bunch, *Jessica Simpson* – who, when asked to name her favorite jeans, allegedly responded *"True Religion"* (with no mention of the jeans sold by the clothing brand … that bears her name.)

Termination Triggers. If an endorsing celebrity does something so heinous that they turn-off their fans and the public in general, what is the value of their endorsement? Accordingly, brand owners have to be able to get out of an endorsement deal and not let a celebrity's negative publicity taint the owner's brand. The classic example is *Lance Armstrong* who, when striped of his *Tour de France* metals after admitting to doping, was unceremoniously dropped by eight (8) brands in a single day, among them - *Nike, Oakley, 24 Hour Fitness* and *RadioShack.* The parameters of acceptable behavior should be spelled out – e.g., will conviction of *any* crime result in termination or must the crime involve an act of *moral turpitude* (something that's dishonest, vile or depraved)?

Social Media & Influencer Arrangements. What role will a celebrity endorser play in the brand's social media presence and identity? These agreements should be based on performance (*e.g.*, increasing traffic to the brand owner's website, creating blog materials that show up in search results, a certain number of *Tweets* within a 120 day period following a product's launch). Again, the agreement must also outline the influencer's obligation to disclose his/her paid relationship to the brand under the *FTC's Truth-in-Advertising* rules discussed in *Chapter 16*.[11] The example that is often used is that of the fashion stylist who recommends (*i.e.*, "endorses") a dress or shoe to her following – *e.g.*, on *YouTube, Instagram, Facebook.* The endorsement might be indirect – e.g., praising craftsmanship and construction, commenting that the price is great bargain and providing a link to the site where the dress can be purchased. If the dress was given to the stylist as compensation for posting the endorsement, the fact that the endorsement was "purchased" – i.e., that the stylist is a paid endorser – must be disclosed to the public.

(C) SPONSORS

Another marketing tool that brand owners use involves the sponsorship of events and venues. The size and nature of the sponsorship is dictated solely by budgetary constraints and the brand owner's values and tastes. For example, a local dress shop can sponsor the neighborhood little league by paying for the team's home uniforms and, in exchange, receiving prominent signage locations – e.g., a banner at the top of the home page on the team's website, a physical sign above the dugout and an embordered logo on the back of the team's shirts.

On the other end of the spectrum, several multi-national corporations spend upwards of $400MM to "brand" well-known buildings and arenas – e.g., *MetLife Stadium* where the *New York Giants* play and *Reliant Stadium,* home of the *Houston Texans.* Similar sponsorship relationships exist in the music industry where, in the 1980s, the *Rolling Stones* and *Michael Jackson* were among the first acts to sign million-dollar tour sponsorships with *Jovan* and *PepsiCo,* respectively. Today, the dollar figures that are spent, e.g., by *Xfinity* as a sponsor of *Taylor Swift's 1989* tour in 2014, are exponentially higher and rising – the dollar amount initially requested in connection with *Adele's* 2015 tour was $30MM.

(D) STRATEGIC ALLIANCE PARTNERS

The *"whole is greater than the sum of its parts"* is the underlying premise in this business relationship between the owners of equally prominent brands which can take many forms. The parties may elect to create a *legally recognized partnership*, a *joint venture* for a specific project or group of projects, or an entirely new *corporate entity.* No matter the form, unless one of the parties contemplates an outright sale and transfer of its trademarks, trade-dress and/or other intellectual property, a strategic alliance will include a license arrangement like the one described in *Chapter 12.*

Examples of creative strategic alliances include *Apple* watches sold with *Hermes* bands, *BMW*'s inclusion of *Monte Blanc* writing and luggage accessories in new vehicles, a commercial for fuel-efficient *Mazda* vehicles that used characters and animated scenery from the *Dr. Seuss* film about environmentalism, the *"Lorax,"* and *Dreamworks Studio's* animation of *IKEA's Lattjo* toy line. In the music industry, innovative personality brand/product alliances created market leaders *Ciroc Vodka, Vitamin Water* and *Beats by Dre* in the spirits, nutritional beverages and electronics industries.

Another way that brands align involves the allocation of loyalty rewards points for the services and products offered by other brands, e.g., *Spotify* subscriptions for frequent *Starbucks* customers, *Shell* gas credits for the purchase of *Kroger* groceries, and in general, the ability to convert *Delta, American, United, SouthWest,* etc. frequent flier airline miles to stays at popular hotel chains like *Marriott, IHG, Carlson, Hilton* and *Wyndham.*

In addition to a license to use each other's trademarks, the agreement between aligned brands spells out each party's contribution in the way of methods/trade secrets, production, marketing, and distribution services. The benefit of a strategic partnership is that each brand provides the other with new opportunities to reach a wider range of customers through enhanced market access. A potential downside of this arrangement is the public's association of the two brands – perhaps inextricably long after the collaborative project has ended.

Chapter 14 Take-Away Notes:

1. ***Three key points to cover in an endorsement arrangements are:***

2. **True or False:** *an effective sponsorship arrangement requires the expenditure of at least $100K and the commitment of a well known celebrity.*

3. ***List organizations and products that might complement, or be complemented by, your brand:***

Sample responses:
stylists and glam/photo shops
dry cleaners and dress shops
parking lots/garages and mobile car detailers
realtors and repair contractors/child-proofers

[11] Like any other product endorsement, social media endorsements are subject to the FTC's *Truth-in-Advertising* laws which include absolute obligations to disclose the fact that the person posting/tweeting, etc. is a paid endorser.

Chapter 15

Product Placement

Also known as *embedded marketing* or *advertising, Product Placement* refers to the promotion of branded goods and services within the context of a music video, television series, film or other visual work. Well-known examples are *Lady Gaga* using *Coca Cola* cans to roller-set her hair in the *"Telephone"* video, the *Manolo Blahnik* pumps with which *Mr. Big* proposed to *Sarah Jessica Parker's* character *Carrie Bradshaw* in *"Sex and the City,"* and the bottle of *Heineken* that a tortured and contemplative *James Bond* consumed while planning his next moves in *"Skyfall."*

Product Placement is basically a way for brands to pay creative content developers a fee in exchange for the ability to reach a target audience – subliminally and in the absence of the channel flipping and "tune-out" associated with traditional commercials. In exchange, the film/video/program owner receives a hefty sum that is often used to offset the cost of production. These amounts range from $15K for placement in a relatively unknown artist's music video on the low end to $50MM for multiple placements in a network television scripted series or a highly anticipated and star-studded studio film. In between, placements in, e.g., non-scripted reality programs and music videos (featuring recognized artists) will cost between $25K to $250K depending on the popularity of the program and the prominence with which the product is featured. *Query*: if social media posts are subject to FTC endorsement disclosure regulations, why aren't de facto product placements on reality TV shows subject to those requirements as well? Insofar as the talent on a reality TV is ... being themselves and ... using particular brands, why isn't that considered an endorsement?

Branded Content (also known as *Branded Entertainment* or *Advertainment*) is, in one respect, the mirror cousin of product placement; brand owners create and produce creative content (e.g., a video, film or series of webisodes) and the content supports and promotes the brands marketing strategy. It differs from other areas of integrated marketing discussed more fully in the next chapter by nuance and intended purpose; whereas *Native Advertising* and *Content Marketing* are designed to inform and educate, the ostensible point of *Branded Content* is to entertain, albeit while delivering the brand owner's pitch in full throttle. *Query*: has society determined where "fake news" falls on the integrated marketing spectrum?

Chapter 15 Take-Away Notes:

1. *List entertainment projects (film, TV, online) that complement or amplify the key components of your brand message (which you identified in Chapters 1 and 2):*

2. *What types of media (in terms of genre and modality) do your customers prefer?*

3. *If a large-scale campaign is out of reach, what types of smaller scale projects exist, e.g., in terms of independent/new film makers, local theater, local programming?*

Chapter 16

Advertising & Marketing Concerns

(A) LOOK BEFORE YOU LEAP - ONTO SHELVES & SCREENS!

Whether you're promoting your brand or lending your name to the promotion of someone else's brand, you should know that advertising, specifically, *"Truth-in-Advertising,"* is an area that is closely monitored and regulated by the *United States Federal Trade Commission* (the "FTC"). In the context of marketing, that agency's focus is not always the obvious advertisements that you see on television; it's often the nebulous area where the line is blurred between honest, disinterested user, on the one hand, and paid influencer/endorser on the other hand (e.g., the social media influencer who is suddenly obsessed with a particular lipstick or pair of shoes).

The FTC also governs the application of the *Children's Online Privacy Protection Act* ("COPPA") which regulates the manner in which information can be collected from and about children. Other areas under the FTC's regulatory framework include labeling requirements for potentially hazardous products ("hazardous" can mean almost anything, from pajamas made from flammable fabrics to small toy-parts that might be swallowed by a child). The disclosure and reporting requirements of the *Consumer Product & Safety Commission* (the "CPSC") govern tangible products that have the potential to injure in the course of ordinary or reasonable use and they fall under the auspices of the FTC as well.

Other agencies that impact marketing/branding efforts and decisions (in terms of timing, compliance/filing costs, etc.) are the *Food & Drug Administration* (the "FDA") for foods and drugs and the *Alcohol Tobacco & Firearms Tax & Trade Bureau* (the "ATF TTB" in connection with products falling under those categories). With regard to cosmetics, it's important to distinguish "drugs" meaning "medicinal" or "pharmaceutical ingredients" which are regulated by the FDA vs. "cosmetics" which generally are not. The following example illustrates the basis for the distinction:

Example: *A fragrance marketed as a way to create allure and enhance attractiveness is a cosmetic. In contrast, a fragrance marketed with "aromatherapy" claims such as assertions that the scent will help the consumer sleep or quit smoking, is considered a drug because of its intended use. Similarly, a massage oil that makes the skin glow or imparts fragrance is generally considered a cosmetic but if the oil is marketed as a cure for muscle pain, it's a drug.* [12]

There are also a number of self-regulated trade organizations wherein specific industries, e.g., advertising/marketing, set their own guidelines for compliance such as the *Child Advertising Review Unit* ("CARU") which reviews and monitors online and traditional advertising geared towards children.

The list will vary depending on your particular industry. For now, suffice it to say that you and your representative should be aware of the need to identify each agency/organization that governs your particular line of business and the corresponding labeling, packaging, marketing, disclosure, etc. requirements that are associated with that business.

(B) Traditional Media

The FTC's rules govern all manner of advertising including traditional commercial advertising on television, on radio and in print. Basically, you can't say or do anything that is untrue or that is likely to mislead consumers. The term "false advertising" sounds archaic in the context of a modern, sophisticated society with constant access to encyclopedic commentary and research. However, therein lies the paradox; because so much information is available from seemingly reliable and authentic sources, the opportunity for abuse and misrepresentation is ever present – though TV, radio and print are not immune, these concerns are exacerbated in the context of online marketing and social media.

(C) Online/Social Media

Facebook, Twitter, Instagram, Pinterest, LinkedIn and the like play a specific role in the marketing campaigns for almost all brands – especially when paid endorsers and influencers share posts/updates regarding the products that they are compensated for using. Similarly, online *Integrated Marketing* strategies are nebulous in that their use as "advertising" isn't always obvious to the consumer. Entire books, websites and associations are devoted to the study and standardization of online marketing and the assignment of terminology is still fluid[13] but common key concepts and terms are summarized below.

- ❖ ***Native Advertising*** is informative content created by a brand owner that conforms to someone else's platform – e.g., *Starbucks promoted* its *Double Shot Expresso* by sponsoring a post about an MIT work/life productivity study in the *Onion,* an online news portal.
- ❖ ***Branded Content*** encompasses content that strives to entertain as opposed to overtly informing; in the context of that "entertainment," the brand owner's products are promoted – e.g., *Porter Magazine,* a beautiful print publication that rivals leading fashion rags *Vogue* and *Harper's Bazaar* was created by online fashion retailer *Net-A-Porter.* Other examples of this form of integrated marketing include the *Lego Movie* (wherein the famous toy was prominently featured) and *Pedigree's* televised radio station ... for dogs.
- ❖ ***Content Marketing*** attracts consumers via the provision of useful information while simultaneously promoting a product – e.g., *Whole Foods* and *Spout's Market* recipes and food cost reduction tips.

While the FTC has been fairly outspoken about disclosure requirements in the context of *Social Media Influencers,*[14] the agency's view of *Integrated Marketing* is still being formulated.[15] The rule of thumb for all advertising applies with equal vigor in this context– if it isn't true, don't say it; if a "real user" has been paid, disclose it; if the message seems the least bit misleading in terms of origin (because of the context and portal of dissemination), at the very least, the brand owner must be disclosed as the source of the message.

In sum, regulatory compliance is an important aspect of marketing your brand (on packaging, in advertisements, via social media) that requires careful attention and review by a qualified attorney *before* your brand is launched.

Chapter 16 Take-Away Notes:

1. ***List three areas of business that are regulated by the FTC:***

2. ***True or false:*** *if you include the word "cosmetic" on a product's label or in its advertising, you still have to comply with FDA regulations.*

3. ***Create a recipe, helpful hint or DIY project that incorporates your product or service. Where and how would you share that useful information as part of an integrated marketing campaign?***

---

[12] See the FDA's guidelines regarding cosmetics at https://www.fda.gov/Cosmetics/GuidanceRegulation/LawsRegulations/ucm074201.htm#Definecosmetic

[13] Esteemed members of the advertising industry have not agreed upon a universal lexicon for the terms referenced above – many of which are often used interchangeably.

[14] https://www.ftc.gov/news-events/press-releases/2016/03/lord-taylor-settles-ftc-charges-it-deceived-consumers

[15] https://www.ftc.gov/tips-advice/business-center/guidance/native-advertising-guide-businesses

PART V

POLICING

Chapter 17

Required Maintenance & Renewal

(A) Trademark Maintenance & Renewal

Your expenses as a registered trademark owner don't end with registration; after the 5th year and before the 6th, you have to file *Declarations* that confirm that you are still using the mark and that it is now "incontestable" (a trademark term meaning "not as vulnerable to challenge" as a new mark would be). You are also required to renew the registration before the end of the 10th year following registration. In order to satisfy the statutory requirements associated with both Maintenance and Renewal, you will have to provide evidence that you are still using your trademark – this the same type of specimen of use covered in Chapter above.

(B) Trademark Watch Services

As a registered trademark owner, you also become responsible for "policing" your mark – i.e., you have to make sure that no one else is using your mark in your area of business without authorization. If they are, and you allow them continue to do so, you compromise the "strength" of your mark (strength refers to consumer "association" discussed in *Chapters 3 and 4* above). As discussed in *Chapter 10,* the extreme example is when a mark becomes so weak (as a result of competitor use) that it becomes generic (e.g., "*Aspirin*" was once an exclusive trademark). One of the ways to ferret out or prevent unauthorized activity is to subscribe to a so-called "watch" or "monitoring" service through your trademark attorney (or other legal representative who is familiar with the process and how to evaluate notices for purposes of determining whether to oppose a conflicting application).

(C) Online Uses, Social Media

You should set up alerts such as *Google Alert* so that the minute you notice someone using any element of your brand (e.g., registered trademarks, photographs of your products, etc.) you can forward a screen shot to your attorney for purposes of sending appropriate notices to the company's legal department and cease and desist letters to the unauthorized user. I reiterate the disclaimer at the beginning of the book: this is ***not*** a DIY manual; always seek and obtain legal counsel before contacting third parties. (You're smart, I know. But you really don't want to risk saying the wrong thing and having it used against you.)

Chapter 17 Take-Away Notes:

1. ***Identify the correct windows for filing post-registration trademark documents:***
   (a) Between years 4 & 5 and 11 & 12.
   (b) Between years 5 & 6 and 9 & 10.
   (c) Between years 2 & 3 and 7 & 8.

2. ***True or false:*** *one way to make sure that your mark remains valid and enforceable is to "watch" it.*

Chapter 18

Oppositions, Cancellations, Enforcement & Customs

(A) PROCEEDINGS IN THE "TTAB" IN GENERAL

The branch of the USPTO that deals with challenges to your application or registration by private parties (i.e., other brand owners) is the *Trademark Trial and Appeal Board* (the "TTAB"). (You'll recall that this is the same branch that hears appeals if the USPTO refuses to accept your application.) If you ever receive an email or letter stating that, e.g., "*your application is being Opposed*" or that "*a Petition has been filed to Cancel*" your existing registration, consult an attorney and get appropriate legal guidance I M M E D I A T E L Y. Time is <u>not</u> your friend when one of these proceedings is initiated against you and missing a deadline can cost you dearly. Similarly, if you receive an alert from your attorney indicating that a competitor has filed an application for a mark that is similar to yours, note that the window for challenging (or opposing) the other brand owner is 30 days; take the call, respond to that email immediately and discuss all pros/cons, likelihood of success and costs (it's litigation, so it's very expensive).

(B) OPPOSITIONS

In *Chapter 3*, we discussed the "*Publication Period*" during which the public has the right to oppose an application listed on the USPTO's Official Gazette and prevent it from being registered. Trademark attorneys review and evaluate published marks via a *Watch or Monitoring Service* (described in *Chapter 17*). If your application is flagged by a private party's attorney during the *Publication Period,* the first thing that you would probably receive is their request to extend the time to file a *Notice of Opposition*. Once it is filed, the clock starts ticking and you (and your attorney) have a limited time to respond.

From there, an opposition matter can either be resolved quickly (e.g., settled in the form of a co-existence agreement) or it can go on ... and on, and on ... sometimes beyond discovery and to trial if the parties can't come to an agreement.

(C) CANCELLATIONS

In *Chapter 17* we discussed the various ongoing maintenance requirements associated with registered marks, including, the *Declaration of Incontestability* that is filed after the 5th anniversary of the registration date and before the 6th. The purposes of that declaration is to make it harder for someone to petition the TTAB to *Cancel* your mark – i.e., to initiate *Cancellation Proceedings*. The usual context for such proceedings is when your registration is cited against someone else's new application to register a similar or identical mark. When the USPTO reviews the new application, they will see your registration and tell the newcomer: *"someone has already obtained (or is in the process of obtaining) a registration for a mark that is identical (or confusingly similar) to yours; so Mr./Ms. Newcomer - your application is rejected."*

In response to the rejection, the newcomer may look for ways to "remove" or "cancel" your registration. If you haven't been using your mark consistently and properly (in the manner described in *Chapter 10*) or if you have allowed others to use it (e.g., via license) without policing and restricting the context in which it is used you are leaving your brand open and vulnerable to attack via cancellation.

(D) ENFORCEMENT

This term covers contentious matters with third parties – either via litigation, arbitration, settlement arrangements. Again, this is not an area you want to DIY. Before you have an opportunity to engage an attorney, whether you're the challenger or the challenge, be careful about what you say and write (either directly or via social media) regarding the matter. The best bet is to refrain from saying, writing, doing ANYTHING until you have an opportunity to speak with your attorney.

(E) U.S. CUSTOMS

Your trademark registration is not automatically recorded with Customs and Boarder Protection, you have to proactively record it for an additional fee. If your mark is used with a product that can be counterfeited, it is wise to take advantage of this entitlement that only registered trademark owners enjoy.

Chapter 18 Take-Away Notes:

1. **True or false:** *the first thing you should do if you receive a claim or cease & desist letter is call the sender.*

2. **True or false:** *the method for objecting to a trademark application that hasn't matured to registration is a Cancellation Proceeding.*

3. ***Once a trademark application is published, the public has ______ days to object to registration:***
   (a) 10
   (b) 25
   (c) 30
   (d) 45

APPENDICES

APPENDIX 3A

OPINION LETTER EXCERPT

RE: INSPIRE HUMAN RESOURCES (WORD MARK); U.S. SEARCH IN INTERNATIONAL CLASS 35 – HUMAN RESOURCES AND RELATED SERVICES.

Dear [Client]:

Per your request, we have conducted a search to determine if there are any pending or registered service marks or trademarks that might interfere with your ability to register and/or use the above-identified mark (the "Subject Mark") in connection with human resources and the provision of related services (e.g., employee training, personnel management) (collectively, the "Subject Services"). The search identifies marks that are pending and/or registered on the Principal Register of the United States Patent and Trademark Office (the "PTO") as well as the registries of the fifty States. In addition, in order to identify non-registrants who may have obtained common law rights in the Subject Mark through prior use, the search also includes the review of information and materials that are accessible via the Internet. A copy of the search report is enclosed for your information and review.[16]

...

Based on the information that you have provided, we can safely assume that an integral part of the Subject Services (*to wit*, "*employee hiring, training, retention and productivity*") will be the provision of instructional services and/or advice on how to "inspire" employees and employers with these goals in mind. Clearly then, the term "inspire," when used in this context, is not fanciful or arbitrary; *i.e.,* it bears some relation to the Subject Services. At the other end of the spectrum, insofar as "inspire" is not a common name for the Subject Services, the mark would not be considered generic. Accordingly, our distinctiveness examination focuses on the fine and often blurred line between a mark that is considered "descriptive" (which requires a showing a secondary meaning) and one that is considered "suggestive" (which does not require a showing of secondary meaning). Two tests have been used to determine whether a particular mark is suggestive or descriptive. The first test focuses on the amount of imagination that a consumer must exercise in order to extract a description of the goods or services from looking at[17] the mark alone; the more imagination the consumer must use, the more likely the mark will be found to be suggestive rather than descriptive. The second test focuses on whether competitors need to use the word in order to accurately describe their own products or services to consumers; if it is not needed, the mark is more likely to be deemed suggestive.

Applying the first test, we note that it would take a good deal of imagination to identify the Subject Services from the word "inspire". Similarly, if we apply the second test we note that competitors' efforts to describe their goods would not be thwarted if they were precluded from using the word "inspire." In view of the foregoing, we believe that the Subject Mark falls within the acceptable definition and scope of suggestive marks.

...

The search identified at least one mark that we thought was worthy of further analysis and discussion – INSPIRE PERFORMANCE.[18] As indicated, this mark is a composite mark like the others. However, it gives us pause because, unlike the others, the balance of this mark (*i.e.*, the word "performance") is arguable descriptive. As such, it has more in common with the Subject Mark. In other words, if this mark was compared side-by-side with the Subject Mark, after disclaiming the phrase "human resources" and the word "performance," the two marks would be identical. Accordingly, we think it prudent to apply the other three factors to analysis of this mark. Focusing on the "similarity of goods" and "similarity of trade channels" questions in tandem, we note that the goods and services that are claimed by the cited applicant, *Centive, Inc.,* are arguably related to the subject goods; *i.e.,* the software applications that *Centive* is selling pertain to "design and management of employee compensation programs.

...

In sum, the marks that we identified in on the PTO website do not appear to preclude your right to seek and obtain registration of the Subject Mark as used in connection with the Subject Services.

[16] For your convenience, and where we believe that it will be helpful to illustrate a point, we direct your attention to certain marks of interest as follows: "*See page 61 of the Search Report.*"
[17] or reading or hearing
[18] *See* citation information above.

APPENDIX 3B

EXCERPT FROM LIST OF INTERNATIONAL TRADEMARK CLASSIFICATIONS

GOODS (PRODUCTS)	
Class 1	**Chemicals** used in industry, … chemical substances for preserving foodstuffs; tanning substances …
Class 2	**Paints** …
Class 3	… cleaning, polishing, scouring and abrasive preparations; non-medicated soaps; perfumery, essential oils, non-medicated **cosmetics**, non-medicated hair lotions …
Class 4	Industrial **oils** and greases; lubricants … **candles** …
Class 5	**Pharmaceuticals**, medical and veterinary preparations; … dietetic food and substances adapted for medical or veterinary use, food for babies; dietary **supplements** for humans and animals …
Class 6	Common **metals** … small items of metal hardware …
Class 7	Machines and **machine tools** …
Class 8	**Hand tools** and implements …
Class 9	… photographic, cinematographic, optical, … **apparatus for recording, transmission or reproduction of sound or images; magnetic data carriers, recording discs; compact discs, DVDs** and other digital recording media; … computers; **computer software** …
Class 10	**Surgical, medical, dental and veterinary apparatus** and instruments …
Class 11	**Apparatus** for **lighting, heating,** steam generating, cooking, refrigerating, drying …

Class 12	**Vehicles** …
Class 13	**Firearms** …
Class 14	**Precious metals** … **jewelry**, precious and semi-precious stones …
Class 15	Musical **instruments**
Class 16	**Paper** … **printed matter** … photographs; stationery … instructional and teaching materials …
Class 17	Unprocessed and semi-processed **rubber** … **plastics** …
Class 18	**Leather** and imitations of leather; animal skins and hides; **luggage and carrying bags** … **collars, leashes and clothing for animals**
Class 19	**Building materials**…
Class 20	**Furniture**, mirrors …
Class 21	Household or **kitchen utensils** and containers; combs and sponges; brushes … glassware, porcelain and earthenware
Class 22	… **raw fibrous textile materials** …
Class 23	**Yarns and threads** …
Class 24	**Textiles** .. **household linen**
Class 25	**Clothing, footwear, headgear**
Class 26	… hair decorations; false **hair**
Class 27	**Carpets** … **wall hangings** (non-textile)
Class 28	**Games, toys** … **sporting articles**; decorations for Christmas trees
Class 29	**Meat**, … **cooked fruits and vegetables; jellies, jams**, compotes; eggs; milk and milk products; edible oils and fats
Class 30	**Coffee, tea, cocoa** … cereals; bread, **pastries and confectionery** … sauces (**condiments**); spices; ice

Class 31	… **raw and unprocessed grains and seeds**; fresh fruits and vegetables, **fresh herbs**; … **foodstuffs and beverages for animals** …
Class 32	**Beers; mineral and aerated waters and other non-alcoholic beverages; fruit beverages and fruit juices** …
Class 33	**Alcoholic beverages (except beers)**
Class 34	**Tobacco; smokers' articles**; matches
SERVICES	
Class 35	**Advertising; business management; business administration**; office functions
Class 36	Insurance; **financial affairs**; monetary affairs; real estate affairs
Class 37	Building **construction**; repair; installation services
Class 38	**Telecommunications**
Class 39	**Transport**; packaging and storage of goods; **travel** arrangement
Class 40	**Treatment** of materials
Class 41	**Education**; providing of training; **entertainment**; **sporting** and cultural activities
Class 42	… research services; **design and development of computer hardware and software**
Class 43	Services for **providing food and drink**; temporary **accommodation**
Class 44	**Medical services**; veterinary services; hygienic and **beauty care** …
Class 45	**Legal services** … **personal and social services rendered by others to meet the needs of individuals**

APPENDIX 3C

EXCERPT FROM SAMPLE RESPONSE TO OFFICE ACTION

IN THE UNITED STATES PATENT AND TRADEMARK OFFICE
EXAMINATION DIVISION

)	IN RE:	APPLICATION OF [DOE]
)	SER. NO.:	87,654321
)	MARK:	[SOMETHING CLEVER]
)		(WORD MARK)
)	EXAMINING ATTORNEY:	[Q.PUBLIC]
)	LAW OFFICE:	123

RESPONSE TO NON-FINAL OFFICE ACTION

I. Overview.

The Applicant respectfully disagrees with the Examining Attorney's decision to refuse registration of the Applicant's mark, ... based, in part, on citation of the mark ... (hereinafter, the "Cited Mark" or the "Cited Registration"). For the reasons set forth below, the Applicant seeks withdrawal of the refusal.

II. There is No Likelihood of Confusion.

A. The *Doctrine of Foreign Equivalents* Does Not Apply.

Under the *Doctrine of Foreign Equivalents*, a foreign word (from a language familiar to an **appreciable segment of American consumers**) and the English equivalent may be held to be confusingly similar. *See, e.g., In re Thomas*, 79 USPQ2d 1021 (TTAB 2006) (emphasis added) (holding MARCHE NOIR for jewelry, and BLACK MARKET MINERALS for retail jewelry and mineral store services, likely to cause confusion); *In re Am. Safety Razor Co.*, 2 USPQ2d 1459 (TTAB 1987) (holding BUENOS DIAS for soap and GOOD MORNING and design for latherless shaving cream likely to cause confusion); *In re Hub Distrib., Inc.*, 218 USPQ 284 (TTAB 1983) (holding EL SOL for clothing and footwear, and SUN and design for footwear, likely to cause confusion).

...

Accordingly, the *Black Market Minerals*, *Good Morning* and *Sun* cases referenced above and cited by the Examining Attorney in the Office Action are simply not on point. The translations in each of those cases were literal and without nuance. In contrast, when the Cited Registration and Applicant's mark are compared, additional steps are required before one them conjures the other; i.e., (i) other, equally pervasive meanings have to be dismissed and (ii) added significance must be imbued in one meaning versus the others. The case at bar is therefor analogous to the *Second Chance* and *Paloma* cases where foreign equivalence, and hence likelihood of confusion, was not found.

...

VI. Conclusion

The Applicant seeks withdrawal of the Examining Attorney's refusal and approval of the Application.

Respectfully submitted,

s/

Attorney for the Applicant

APPENDIX 4A

SAMPLE WORK FOR HIRE AGREEMENT

SoulGlo Hair Care, Inc.
123 Mockingbird Lane
Anytown, USA 86793

Dates as of the ____ of ___, 20__

[Name/address of contractor]

Dear ________________

In exchange for good and valuable consideration, the sufficiency of which is hereby acknowledged, the parties hereto agree to and confirm the following understanding between you and ***SoulGlo Hair Care, Inc.*** regarding work to be done by you as more fully described below:

[insert a description of services to be rendered by independent contractor, e.g., marketing consultation, videography, graphic design, music/jingle production] (hereinafter, the "Work").

1. You agree to deliver the Work to us no later than ______ __, 20__ in a manner and form that is satisfactory to us.

2. Within ten (10) business days of our acceptance of the Work, we agree to pay you the sum of ________ Dollars ($___) in exchange for which you hereby grant and assign any and all rights in the Work, throughout the Universe, in perpetuity, whether such rights are now known or hereinafter discovered. You will not receive any further payment from us.

3. You expressly acknowledge that the material contributed by you hereunder, and your services hereunder, are being specially ordered and commissioned by us for use in connection

with [*name of project*]. The Work, and any constituent elements thereof, shall be considered a "work made for hire" as defined by the copyright laws of the United States. We shall be the sole and exclusive owner and copyright proprietor of all rights and title in and to the results and proceeds of your services hereunder in whatever stage of completion. If for any reason the results and proceeds of your services hereunder are determined at any time not to be a "work made for hire", you hereby irrevocably transfer and assign to us all right, title and interest therein, including all copyrights, as well as all renewals and extensions thereto.

4. You agree that we may make any changes or additions to the Work prepared by you, which we in our sole discretion may consider necessary, and may engage others to do any or all of the foregoing, with or without attribution to you. You further agree to waive any so-called moral rights in the Work.

5. You represent that, except with respect to material furnished to you by us, you are the sole author of the Work and all of your services are original with you and not copied in whole or in part from any other work. You further represent that your Work is not libelous or obscene, or a violation of the right of privacy or publicity, or any other rights of any person, firm or entity.

If the above reflects your understanding, please sign below to reflect your agreement to the above terms and your intention to be bound hereby.

Sincerely,

SOULGLO HAIR CARE, INC.

AGREED AND ACCEPTED:

[*contractor's name*]

APPENDIX 4B

APPEARANCE CONSENT & RELEASE FORM

Consent and Release – Acme Training Materials and Uses

I, ____________________________________, herby grant ***Acme Productions, Inc.*** ("***Acme***") permission to use, exploit, adapt, modify, reproduce, distribute, publicly perform, display, transmit, broadcast in any form now known or later developed, my image, visual likeness, name, voice, and other element of my persona (collectively, "My Persona") throughout the world by incorporating it into an audio-visual work for the purposes of training ***Acme*** employees and franchisees and producing related materials including, without limitation, related sound recordings, compositions, advertisements, social media, publications, websites, magazines, exhibits, films, videos, photographs, brochures, books, magazines, blogs, online portals or references of any kind and/or other media, whether now known or later invented (collectively, the "Works").

I waive any right to inspect or approve the Works. I understand that ***Acme*** shall be the exclusive owner of all right, title and interest, including copyright, in the Works and that I shall not receive any royalty or payment in connection with the Works.

I represent and warrant that nothing contained in My Persona is or will be owned or controlled by any third party and/or that the use of My Persona as contemplated is fully authorized by any such third party. I release and agree to defend and hold harmless ***Acme*** its agents, employees, licensees, assigns and designees from and against any and all claims I or any third party may have now, or in the future for invasion of privacy, right of publicity, right of attribution/authorship, copyright/trademark/patent infringement, defamation, or any other cause of action arising out of the use, exploitation, reproduction, adaption, distribution, broadcast, performance or display of My Persona.

I hereby release and agree to defend and hold harmless ***Acme*** its agents, employees, licensees, assigns and designees from and against any liability, claims, or causes of action of <u>any</u> kind, resulting or arising from the use of My Persona.

Acme shall have the right to use My Persona in connection with the Works and the scope of the waivers, consents, and permissions that I have granted are ongoing and not dependent on my status as an employee or non-employee of BYB at the time of publication or other use of the Works.

I HAVE READ THIS RELEASE AND WAIVER OF LIABILITY, UNDERSTAND ITS TERMS AND I HAVE SIGNED IT FREELY AND VOLUNTARILY. I ACKNOWLEDGE THAT I HAVE EITHER SOUGHT INDEPENDENT LEGAL COUNSEL WHO HAS INTERPRETED THE PROVISIONS OF THIS RELEASE OR I HAVE WAIVED MY RIGHT TO DO SO.

Team Member:

_____(Printed)_____(Signature)_____(Date)

If Team Member is a Minor:
Parent/Guardian:

_____(Printed)_____(Signature)_____(Date)

Appendix 4C

Non-Disclosure / Confidentiality Agreement

NON-DISCLOSURE AGREEMENT

THIS AGREEMENT (the "**Agreement**") is entered into on __________ _____, ____and is between ***Nunaya Corp***., a Delaware corporation ("**Disclosing Party**"), and the undersigned ("***Recipient***"). Disclosing Party and Recipient entered into that certain agreement regarding marketing services on May 25, 2016 (the "**Agreement**"). In consideration of the mutual promises and covenants contained in the Agreement, this Agreement, and other good and valuable consideration, the receipt and sufficiency of which is hereby acknowledged, the parties hereto agree as follows:

1. **General.** Recipient agrees to keep the Confidential Information (as defined below) strictly confidential. Without limiting the generality of the foregoing, Recipient shall: **(a)** limit disclosure of Confidential Information to its employees (collectively, "**Employees**") who have a need-to-know such Confidential Information in furtherance of Recipient's duties under the Agreement, and only for that purpose; **(b)** advise its Employees of the proprietary nature of the Confidential Information and of the obligations set forth in this Agreement, and require such Employees to keep the Confidential Information strictly confidential; **(c)** not disclose any Confidential Information received by it to any third parties (except as expressly provided for in subsection (b) herein); and **(d)** use the Confidential Information solely in furtherance of its obligations under the Agreement and not for any other purpose. Disclosing Party is responsible for any breach by any of its Employees of the obligations contained in this section.

2. **Definition of Confidential Information.** "**Confidential Information**" means any information that is proprietary to Disclosing Party, or that is not generally known to the public, whether in tangible or intangible form, including, but not limited to: **(a)** the existence of this Agreement and all terms and conditions of the proposed Agreement; **(b)** Disclosing Party's marketing plans, plans for new products, financial data, projections, sales, business plans and performance results; supplier lists and information regarding suppliers; designs, procedures, recipes and methods; and **(c)** any other information regarding Disclosing Party that should reasonably be recognized as confidential information of Disclosing Party. Notwithstanding the foregoing, Confidential Information shall not include information which: **(i)** was known by or independently developed by Recipient prior to receiving the Confidential Information; **(ii)** becomes known to Recipient from a third-party source not under an obligation of confidentiality; or **(iii)** is or becomes publicly available through no fault of Recipient.

3. **Exceptions.** Notwithstanding anything herein to the contrary, Recipient may disclose Confidential Information pursuant to any governmental, judicial or administrative order, subpoena, or similar request, provided that, if not legally prohibited, Recipient promptly notifies Disclosing Party in writing of such demand for disclosure so that Disclosing Party, at its sole expense, may seek to limit such disclosure or other appropriate remedy to preserve the confidentiality of the Confidential Information.

4. **Term.** This Agreement shall remain in effect for a period of three years from the date that the Agreement expires. Notwithstanding the foregoing, the duty to hold in confidence Confidential Information that constitutes a trade secret shall remain in effect indefinitely.

5. **Remedies.** Recipient acknowledges that the Confidential Information to be disclosed hereunder is of a unique and valuable character, and that the unauthorized dissemination of the Confidential Information would destroy or diminish the value of such information. The damages to Disclosing Party that would result from the unauthorized dissemination of the Confidential Information would be impossible to calculate. Therefore, Recipient agrees that Disclosing Party shall be entitled to injunctive relief preventing the dissemination of any Confidential Information in violation of the terms hereof. Such injunctive relief shall be in addition to any other remedies available hereunder, whether at law or in equity. Disclosing Party shall be entitled to recover its costs and fees, including reasonable attorneys' fees, incurred in obtaining any such relief. Further, in the event of litigation relating to this Agreement, the prevailing party, shall be entitled to recover its reasonable attorney's fees and expenses.

6. **Return of Confidential Information.** Upon Disclosing Party's request, Recipient shall immediately **(a)** return or destroy all tangible material embodying the Confidential Information provided hereunder and all tangible notes, summaries, memoranda, drawings, manuals, records, excerpts or derivative information deriving therefrom and all other documents or materials; **(b)** delete all Confidential Information that exists in an electronic form; and **(c)** Recipient shall provide a certification signed by an officer of Recipient that the actions set forth in subsections (a) and (b) have been taken.

7. **Miscellaneous.** **(a)** This Agreement constitutes the entire understanding between the parties and supersedes any and all prior or contemporaneous understandings and agreements, whether oral or written, between the parties, with respect to the subject matter hereof. This Agreement can only be modified by a written amendment signed by the party against whom enforcement of such modification is sought. **(b)** The validity, construction and performance of this Agreement shall be governed and construed in accordance with the laws of the state of Tennessee principal place of business, without giving effect to any conflict of laws provisions thereof. Federal and state courts located nearest to Disclosing Party's principal place of business shall have sole and exclusive jurisdiction over any disputes arising under this Agreement. **(c)** Any failure by either party to enforce the other party's strict performance of any provision of this Agreement will not constitute a waiver of its right to subsequently enforce such provision or any other provision of this Agreement. **(d)** Although the restrictions contained in this Agreement are considered by the parties to be reasonable for the purpose of protecting the Confidential Information, if any such restriction is found by a court of competent jurisdiction to be unenforceable, such provision will be modified, rewritten or interpreted to include as much of its nature and scope as will render it enforceable. **(e)** This Agreement may be executed in counterparts, each of which shall be deemed an original and both of which taken together shall constitute one and the same document.

IN WITNESS WHEREOF, the parties hereto have executed this Agreement as of the date first above written.

APPENDIX 6A

EXAMPLE OF CONSENT OF LIVING INDIVIDUAL FOR TRADEMARK USE OF NAME / PSEUDONYM

IN THE UNITED STATES PATENT AND TRADEMARK OFFICE TRADEMARK EXAMINING OPERATION

Commissioner for Trademarks
P.O Box 1451
Alexandria, VA 22313-1451

CONSENT TO USE OF NAME OF LIVING INDIVIDUAL
IN ACCORDANCE WITH TRADEMARK ACT SECTION 2(C), 15 U.S.C. § 1052(C)

I, *Jayne B. Doe*, in my individual capacity and as a principal of *Doe Taxidermy & Haberdashery, Inc.*, hereby affirm:

(a) The name, DOE A DEER LADY, is a pseudonym that identifies the undersigned, *Jayne B. Doe*, a living individual whose consent to register is made of record; and

(b) I consent to the use and registration by *Doe Taxidermy & Haberdashery, Inc*. of my name, DOE A DEER LADY as a trademark and/or service mark with the USPTO.

Sincerely,

Jayne B. Doe

(on behalf of Doe Taxidermy & Haberdashery, Inc. and in my individual capacity)
Dated:______________

APPENDIX 7A

EXAMPLES OF USPTO EVALUATION OF ONLINE-WEBSITE SPECIMENS FOR GOODS/PRODUCTS

USPTO TMEP §904.03(i)(B)(2)

Accepted Trademark Specimens:

https://tmep.uspto.gov/RDMS/TMEP/current#/current/ch900_d1fd02_1d58b_173.html

Subject Mark: BROOKS BROTHERS
Subject Goods: Bed sheets, dust ruffles, duvet covers, pillow cases, pillow shams, bed shams, bed spreads, towels, and wash cloths.
Basis for Acceptance:

- Subject Mark is displayed prominently in large font and placed above the pictures of the goods.
- No other marks are displayed in connection with the claimed goods other than a sheep logo design that is also associated with the goods.
- Screen shot contains pictures and descriptions of the goods, available sizes/colors and pricing information.

USPTO TMEP §904.03(i)(B)(2) and (C)

Rejected Trademark Specimens:

HTTPS://TMEP.USPTO.GOV/RDMS/TMEP/CURRENT#/CURRENT/TMEP-900D1E882.HTML

Subject Mark: LEADING EDGE TONERS
Subject Goods: Numerous goods including toner, toner cartridges, ink sticks, components for laser toner cartridges, and printer parts
Basis for Rejection:

- Use in the URL only identifies the website where retail services are conducted; does not show use in connection with the Subject Goods.
- The mark functions as a service mark for retail store or distributorship services, but it doesn't function as a trademark because it appears in the upper-left corner of the web page where service marks normally appear and there are other marks used in connection with the goods.
- Subject Mark used with third-party trademarks (e.g., "*Leading Edge Toners Best Prices for Tektronix Toners*") supports applicant's services a retail store / distributor, does not support claim for toner – the Subject Goods.

APPENDIX 7B –

EXAMPLE OF ONLINE SPECIMENS FOR SERVICES

USPTO TMEP §1301.04(i)

Accepted Service Mark Specimens

HTTPS://TMEP.USPTO.GOV/RDMS/TMEP/CURRENT#/CURRENT/CH1300_D2266F_1DCC2_11C.HTML

Subject Mark: HOMETOWN SOUNDS
Subject Services: Electronic transmission and streaming of digital media ... in Class 38.
Basis for Acceptance:

- Shows the mark used in providing the services.
- Subject Mark is displayed in large font at top of webpage.
- The following statements:
  - *"DC's local music internet station" describes the services.*
  - *"Listen Now"*
  - *"Click Here to listen to Hometown Sounds".*
- It is customary to display service marks near the top of the webpage where they are advertised, accessed, rendered, and experienced. The Subject Mark appears above references to the services and instructions for accessing the services.

USPTO TMEP §1301.04(j)

Rejected Service Mark Specimen

HTTPS://TMEP.USPTO.GOV/RDMS/TMEP/CURRENT#/CURRENT/CH1300_D22670_19203_1C6.HTML

Mark: IObit
Services: Computer programming ... maintenance of computer software, in Class 42.
Basis for Rejection:

- The following statements did not describe services:
  - *"Our sincere commitment to all our customers is that we will continue delivering ...."*
  - *"We pursue the genuine ambition of ...."*
- It is unclear whether the reference to "online service" is to a separate service or part of the free software goods.
- A reference to becoming a "top utility producer and Windows system service provider" is not sufficient to indicate actually being a provider of the identified services.

GLOSSARY

Cancellation	Process whereby a Petition is filed to cancel an existing Registration.
Clearance	The process by which a mark is searched and evaluated for availability and the ability to register and protect it.
Copyright	exclusive right of the creator of literary, artistic, musical or other creative work to publish, sell, distribute and/or perform the work publicly.
Descriptiveness	Term used to describe marks that merely describe an element, feature, component, function, etc. of the owner's products or services.
Design Patent	Protects the non-functional ("random") elements of a article. Similar
***Ex Parte* Appeal**	If a Trademark Examiner maintains a refusal (e.g., for descriptiveness, likelihood of confusion, etc.), you can appeal their finding.
First to File	Refers to the ideology of some countries outside the U.S. (e.g., China), where, unlike the U.S. which basis registration on proven use of a mark, the first person (or company) to file is entitled to registration.
Functionality	A basis for refusing registration in the USPTO in the context of Trade Dress; when the feature for which protection is sought serves an actual purpose or function (e.g., a zipper).
Intent to Use ("ITU" or "1B")	A basis for applying for trademark registration before the mark is in use which is permitted under section 1(b) of the Trademark Act.
Mark	Another term for a "trademark."
Likelihood of Confusion	A basis for refusal where a previously filed Application or Registration is cited against the current Application.
Madrid Filing	A mechanism for expanding a U.S. Trademark Registration to multiple countries.

Opposition	A proceeding whereby a more senior Trademark Applicant or Registrant can object to and prevent registration of a newer Applicant.
Ornamentation	A basis for refusal stemming from lack of trademark use, e.g., submission of Specimens of Use that show a mark on the front of a shirt and not on a label, hang-tag or on a website where the shirts are sold.
Principal Register	Part of the USPTO Trademark registry that confers the most extensive rights; granted to trademark owners of marks that are currently in use in interstate/international commerce that have been approved by the Trademark Examining Unit..
Priority Rights	Last for 6 months from the date that a U.S. Application is filed; during that time, it is advantageous to file in other countries and use the date of the U.S. Application as the constructive filing date.
Protectability	Spectrum by which potential marks are evaluated based on the degree to which the law protects e.g., Arbitrary, Fanciful, Suggestive marks and precludes exclusive rights in Descriptive marks and Generic terms.
Publication	The 30 day period following examination and approval of a Trademark Application during which the owners of already filed/registered marks can Oppose an Application.
Recordation	When a trademark application or registration is assigned to another person or company, the assignment document (e.g., an exhibit to a license agreement) must be recorded with the Trademark Office.
Service Mark ("SM")	Same as a Trademark but used with services (e.g., an entertainment establishment, special events planner, fashion stylist – all provide services).

SECONDARY MEANING	When consumers attribute an otherwise descriptive element of a trademark (e.g., a word, design, shape/packaging of a product) to a single owner.
SPECIMENS OF USE	Required in order to show the USPTO that an applied-for Trademark or Service Mark is actually in use in interstate or international commerce.
SUPPLEMENTAL REGISTER	The part of the USPTO Trademark Registry that is reserved for marks that are initially viewed as descriptive or functional which are nevertheless capable of becoming source indicators for the brand owner in the future.
TRADEMARK ("TM")	Anything that functions as an indicator of origin for a particular product (e.g., a word, design, smell, color, sound) in the marketplace.
TRADE DRESS	The visual appearance of a product or its packaging that signify the source of the product to consumers.
TTAB	Trademark Trial & Appeal Board (where *Ex Parte* Appeals, Oppositions, Cancellations are filed).
THREE SIXTY ("360") DEAL	Type of agreement where rights that are ancillary to the subject matter of the agreement are implicated

ABOUT THE AUTHOR

Christine C. Washington has practiced intellectual property law as a member of the New York Bar since 1994. She's a graduate of Howard University (Bachelor of Business Administration - Marketing), Duke University (Juris Doctorate) and New York University (Master of Laws in Intellectual Property) and a member of the International Trademark Association (INTA). Prior to joining the legal profession, Christine's work experiences centered around corporate marketing and media relations. As a practicing attorney, she has worked in the in-house and law firm environments where she's represented high-profile brand leaders in all industries, worldwide.

For contact information, please visit
www.MarksForMusicMoviesAndMore.com

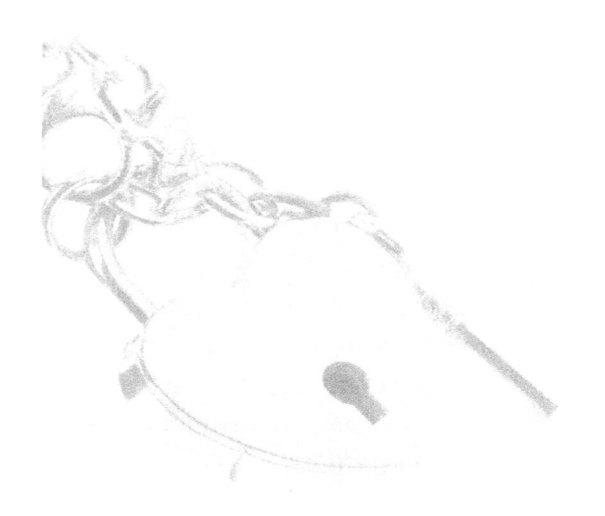

Made in the USA
Monee, IL
10 May 2020

30225832R00115